ACROSS THE LINES

A Reflective Memoir on Race, Leadership, and Human Dignity

By Dan Dressman, Ed.D.

Dedication

To my wife Donna and our family, whose encouragement made this journey possible, and to all those whose lives and stories have helped broaden my understanding of humanity. I hope that my story encourages our grandchildren, Oliver, Benny, and Ramona, to continue crossing the lines to promote harmony and justice in the world. Thanks to Clara, who was the initial inspiration for this book.

"We must learn to live together as brothers or perish together as fools."
— Martin Luther King, Jr.

Author's Note

I did not set out to write a book about race.

For most of my life, the experiences described in these pages unfolded quietly, one relationship and one moment at a time. They were simply part of the path my life happened to take—growing up in Covington, Kentucky, building a career in housing and association leadership, navigating recovery through Alcoholics Anonymous, raising a family, and eventually teaching business leadership to university students.

Only later did I begin to recognize that many of those experiences shared a common thread. Again and again, my life had brought me into contact with people whose backgrounds, cultures, and life circumstances differed from my own. Each encounter offered an opportunity to see the world from a slightly different perspective.

Over time, those perspectives accumulated into a larger understanding.

This book grew out of that realization. I wrote it now for two reasons.

First, after more than four decades of professional leadership, community involvement, and personal recovery, I have had enough distance to reflect on the experiences that shaped my thinking. Many of the lessons described here were not immediately clear when they occurred. It took years—and sometimes decades—for their meaning to become fully visible.

Second, our country continues to wrestle with questions about race, opportunity, and justice. Conversations about these topics often become polarized, with people speaking past one another rather than listening.

This book is not an attempt to resolve those debates.

Instead, it is simply the story of one person's journey of learning.

My perspective is shaped by the life I have lived: that of a White man raised in a large, middle-class Catholic family, working in industries that historically lacked diversity, and later becoming part of communities—through recovery, leadership, faith, and education—where people from very different backgrounds came together with a shared purpose.

Along the way, I learned that understanding rarely comes from grand theories alone. It often grows through relationships. Through listening to the experiences of others. Through moments when we recognize that the boundaries separating us are sometimes far thinner than we imagined.

Readers approaching this book may find that some parts resonate with their own experiences, while other parts may challenge their assumptions. That is perfectly natural. My hope is not that every reader will agree with every reflection, but that the story encourages thoughtful consideration of how each of us encounters difference in our own lives.

The journey described here is not a finished one. Like most people, I am still learning.

And perhaps that is the most important lesson of all: understanding is not something we arrive at once and for all. It is something we continue developing as we encounter new people, new perspectives, and new opportunities to grow.

If this book encourages even a small number of readers to approach those encounters with curiosity and empathy, then it will have served its purpose.

I recognize that conversations about race and identity involve complex histories and perspectives. The reflections in this book represent one individual's personal journey of learning and understanding.

This book is a work of narrative nonfiction based on the author's life experiences. Some names, identifying characteristics, and details have been changed to protect the privacy of individuals. Any resemblance to actual persons, living or deceased, beyond those intentionally identified, is coincidental.

The views and reflections expressed in this book represent the personal experiences and perspectives of the author. They are offered to encourage thoughtful dialogue and personal reflection and are not intended as definitive statements about any individual, organization, or community.

Every effort has been made to ensure the accuracy of the information presented in this book. However, the author and publisher make no representations or warranties with respect to the completeness or accuracy of the contents and specifically disclaim any implied warranties of merchantability or fitness for a particular purpose.

Neither the author nor the publisher shall be liable for any loss or damage arising from the use of the information contained in this book.

This book is intended for educational and reflective purposes only.

Published by
Dressman Strategies, LLC
Bellevue, KY, USA

For information about bulk purchases, speaking engagements, or educational use, please contact:
www.dressmanstrategies.com

ISBN: 979-8-9949818-3-2 (Paperback)
ISBN: 979-8-9949818-4-9 (eBook)
Library of Congress Control Number: 2026907104

Printed in the United States of America

First Edition

Requests for permission to reproduce material from this work should be directed to:

Permissions Department
Dressman Strategies, LLC
www.dressmanstrategies.com

Interior design, cover design, and production assistance by the author, with editorial support tools.

Scripture quotations, if any, are taken from the New Revised Standard Version of the Bible unless otherwise noted.

Foreword

Stories have the power to shape how we see the world. They challenge assumptions, illuminate experiences beyond our own, and sometimes invite us to reconsider what we thought we understood about ourselves and others.

In this reflective narrative, I offer readers a personal journey through decades of learning about race, leadership, faith, and the shared dignity of humanity. My story does not begin with dramatic activism or academic theory. Instead, it begins with small moments—childhood observations, simple questions, and encounters with people whose lives gradually broadened my perspective.

What makes this story meaningful is its honesty. I do not claim expertise in the complex subject of race in America. Rather, I present myself as a lifelong learner, someone whose understanding developed through relationships, professional experiences, and the humbling lessons of recovery.

From Alcoholics Anonymous meetings to boardrooms, classrooms, and service trips across the country, my experiences illustrate a powerful truth: real understanding grows through relationships.

In a time when discussions about race can quickly become polarized, this narrative reminds us that empathy and awareness often emerge through simple human encounters. It is through listening, humility, and curiosity that individuals—and societies—begin to grow.

The reflections in this book invite readers to examine their own experiences and consider how their lives intersect with the lives of others.

Table of Contents

Introduction

If you had asked me as a young boy growing up in Covington, Kentucky, what I understood about race in America, my answer would have been simple: not much.

Like many White Americans of my generation, race was something I occasionally heard about on the evening news or studied briefly in history classes. It seemed like an issue connected to other places and other people. It did not feel like something that shaped my everyday life.

Looking back now, I realize that race was present in my life from the very beginning. I simply did not yet have the awareness to recognize it.

My journey toward understanding race did not begin with a dramatic moment of revelation. Instead, it unfolded slowly over decades through a series of experiences, relationships, and observations that gradually reshaped how I saw the world.

Many of those lessons came through ordinary encounters, conversations with friends, experiences in the workplace, moments in recovery meetings, and interactions with people whose lives were very different from my own.

Each of those moments widened my perspective. Some challenged assumptions I did not even realize I held. Others revealed how deeply history and culture shape the opportunities people encounter throughout their lives.

This book is not meant to be an academic analysis of race relations in America. Many scholars and historians are far better equipped to provide that kind of examination. Instead, this book is my personal story. It is the story of how one person's understanding of race, dignity, leadership, and faith evolved over the course of a lifetime.

My hope is that these reflections encourage readers to consider their own journeys and to remain open to the lessons that come from stepping beyond familiar boundaries. Understanding rarely arrives all at once. It grows gradually. Often, through relationships that may be similar, or different.

The journey described in this book unfolds across several stages of life, each shaped by experiences that gradually expanded my understanding of race, leadership, faith, and human dignity.

Rather than presenting a historical analysis or academic argument, this memoir traces how perspective often develops slowly through relationships, encounters, and moments of reflection. The chapters are organized in a way that mirrors that personal journey.

Chapter 1

Clara, Covington, and the Invisible Lines

Clara was an older Black woman who came to our home once each week when I was growing up.

My parents had twelve children, and managing a household of that size required help. Clara arrived by bus, the fare provided by my mother—and spent the day assisting with laundry, cleaning, and sometimes cooking.

She carried herself with quiet confidence. She was cheerful, soft-spoken, and patient with all of us children. Looking back now, I realize how remarkable her composure must have been in a house filled with the constant noise and energy of twelve siblings.

At the time, however, she was simply part of our weekly routine.

But as a curious young boy, I often wondered about her life outside our home. Where did she live? Did she have children of her own? What was her neighborhood like?

Those questions drifted through my mind occasionally, but I never asked them. That silence reflects something important about how many children of my generation grew up. We often interacted with people from different backgrounds, yet rarely took the step of learning their stories.

Clara arrived in the morning. She worked throughout the day.

Then she boarded the bus and disappeared back into a world we knew nothing about. Looking back, I realize that curiosity without action has limits.

I wondered about Clara's life, but I never asked her about it. That silence reflected more than childhood innocence. It reflected a broader pattern—one that existed in many communities at the time. People could live alongside one another, interact regularly, even depend on each other, and yet never fully know one another's stories.

The distance was not always physical. Often, it was conversational. And sometimes, it was unintentional. But it was real.

Clara was one of the first people who piqued my curiosity. It would take years before I learned how to turn that curiosity into understanding.

Our neighborhood in Covington, Kentucky, was mostly White. A few Black households existed nearby, but most Black residents lived north of 13th Street. That boundary was never formally announced. There were no signs marking it, no maps handed out to explain it. And yet, even as a child, I sensed that it was there.

An invisible line. Children notice more than we often give them credit for. I could see the difference between the two areas, even if I didn't yet have the language to describe it. The homes in our neighborhood appeared better maintained. Lawns were trimmed. The paint was fresh. The streets felt orderly, predictable.

Crossing north of 13th Street, something changed. The houses looked different. The streets felt different. The overall environment carried a different tone—one I couldn't fully explain but could clearly feel.

At that age, I didn't interpret those differences through the lens of history or policy. I saw them simply as facts—two neighborhoods that did not look the same. And like most children, I turned to the person I trusted most to help me make sense of what I was seeing.

One day, I asked my mother a simple question. "Why don't the houses in the Black neighborhood look as nice as ours?" Her answer was direct. Matter of fact. Without hesitation. "They're poor," she said. "They can't afford better houses."

At the time, that explanation seemed logical. It fit neatly into the way a child understands the world—simple cause and effect. Some people have more. Some people have less. That was enough to satisfy my curiosity, at least for the moment.

Children often accept the answers they are given without questioning the larger forces behind them. And so, I did. I moved on. Played with friends. Rode my bike. Continued growing up within a framework I didn't yet know was incomplete. It would take many years before I began to understand how much was missing from that explanation.

What I had seen as a child was not just differences in income or individual circumstance. They were the visible outcomes of deeper, more complex forces—forces that had been shaping American cities long before I was born.

Housing patterns were not accidental. They were influenced by policies like redlining, where banks and federal programs systematically denied loans to Black families in certain neighborhoods. They were shaped by restrictive covenants that prevented Black families from purchasing homes in many areas. They reflected decades of segregation—both legal and informal—that limited where people could live, work, and build wealth.

Opportunities were not distributed evenly. Access to quality schools, stable employment, and financial resources often followed the same invisible lines that divided neighborhoods. Over time, those patterns reinforced themselves, creating cycles that were difficult to break. But none of that was visible to a young boy growing up in the 1960s.

There were no conversations about systemic inequality at the dinner table. No discussions about housing policy or economic disparity. No framework to connect what I saw with the broader story of how those conditions came to be. What I saw instead were neighborhoods that appeared different. What I believed was that those differences were simply the result of individual circumstances.

What I did not yet understand was why. Looking back, I recognize that moment—asking my mother that question—as an early encounter with something much larger than I could comprehend at the time.

It was a moment where observation met explanation. And the explanation, although not unkind, was incomplete. That incompleteness matters. Because the way we explain the world to children often becomes the foundation for how they understand it as adults. Simple answers can unintentionally mask complex truths. They can shift attention away from systems and place it solely on individuals.

It would take years—through education, relationships, and lived experience—before I began to see beyond that initial explanation. To ask different questions. To listen more carefully.
To recognize patterns that had once been invisible to me. The line that ran through Covington was never marked on a map.

But it was real. It shaped where people lived.
It influenced what they had access to. It quietly reinforced differences that seemed, on the surface, to be natural or inevitable. As a child, I could see the line. As an adult, I began to understand it.

And that understanding would become an important part of a much larger journey—one that challenged me to look beyond appearances and to ask not just *what is different*, but *why those differences exist.*

To better understand the world many Americans experienced during the 1960s, it helps to step back for a moment and consider the larger forces shaping the country at that time. For children growing up in neighborhoods like mine in Covington, Kentucky, life often appeared stable and familiar. Families attended church, children went to school, and communities developed rhythms that felt predictable and orderly.

Yet beneath that surface, the United States was undergoing one of the most significant social transformations in its history. The Civil Rights Movement was challenging long-standing systems of racial separation and inequality that had existed for generations.

For many Americans, these changes were visible primarily through television images and newspaper headlines. For others—particularly Black Americans—the changes affected nearly every aspect of daily life.

Understanding that national backdrop helps explain why the "invisible lines" I noticed as a child were not accidental. They were the result of decades of laws, policies, and social practices that had shaped where people lived, where children attended school, and what opportunities were available to different communities.

One of the most important turning points came in 1964 when Congress passed the Civil Rights Act.

The law prohibited discrimination based on race, color, religion, sex, or national origin in many areas of public life. It outlawed segregation in public accommodations such as hotels, restaurants, theaters, and other facilities that had long been divided along racial lines.

For decades before that moment, segregation had been embedded in many aspects of American society, particularly in the South but also in parts of the Midwest and North.

The Civil Rights Act marked a national commitment to dismantling those systems. While the law represented a major step forward, passing legislation did not instantly erase generations of inequality. In many places, the practical effects of segregation continued through customs, economic disparities, and community resistance to change.

Still, the Act signaled a profound shift in the direction of American law and public policy. Education became another major arena for change.

In 1954, the Supreme Court's decision in Brown v. Board of Education declared that racially segregated public schools were unconstitutional. The ruling overturned decades of legal precedent that had allowed separate schools for Black and White students.

Despite that landmark decision, integration did not happen quickly. In many communities, school districts resisted implementing the ruling. Some states adopted policies designed to delay integration, while others closed public schools rather than comply.

Across the country, children sometimes found themselves at the center of intense national debates.

Television images from the late 1950s and early 1960s showed federal troops escorting Black students into previously all-White schools. Those moments became powerful symbols of the struggle to ensure equal educational opportunities.

Even in places where schools were technically integrated, the legacy of earlier housing patterns often meant that classrooms remained largely divided along neighborhood lines. Housing patterns played a major role in shaping American communities.

For much of the twentieth century, many cities were structured by policies that limited where Black families could live. Banks, insurance companies, and real estate practices often reinforced these patterns.

One widely documented practice was redlining—the practice of marking certain neighborhoods, often those with significant Black populations, as high-risk for mortgage lending. Residents in those areas frequently struggled to obtain home loans or property insurance.

The result was a cycle that reinforced inequality. Neighborhoods denied investment often experienced slower development and fewer economic opportunities.

In 1968, Congress passed the Fair Housing Act, which prohibited discrimination in the sale, rental, and financing of housing based on race, religion, national origin, and later, other characteristics.

Like the Civil Rights Act before it, the Fair Housing Act represented an effort to remove legal barriers that had restricted opportunities for many families. But the physical patterns created by earlier policies did not disappear overnight. Many cities continued to reflect those earlier divisions long after the law changed.

As a child growing up in Covington, I did not understand the historical forces shaping our community. I simply noticed that neighborhoods looked different. Some areas had well-maintained homes, stable property values, and access to resources like parks and quality schools. Other areas struggled with aging infrastructure, limited investment, and fewer opportunities.

What I did not realize yet was that those differences were often connected to decades of public policy and economic practice. Urban neighborhoods across the country had developed patterns that reflected both opportunity and exclusion.

These patterns influenced where families lived, where children went to school, and what kinds of jobs and resources were available in different parts of a city. For many Americans, those patterns created invisible boundaries—lines that separated communities not only by geography but also by opportunity.

As a child, I did not yet have the perspective to understand those broader dynamics. The differences I observed between neighborhoods seemed simple and straightforward. When I asked my mother why some homes looked different from others, her answer—that some families were poor—seemed logical enough.

It would take many years before I began to understand how incomplete that explanation really was. Economic inequality, housing policy, school systems, and long-standing social traditions had all contributed to shaping the communities around me.

The result was a country in the midst of change. The 1960s became a decade when many Americans began confronting the distance between the ideals expressed in the nation's founding documents and the realities experienced by many of its citizens.

Some people responded to those challenges with courage and determination. Others resisted the changes or struggled to understand them. For a young boy growing up in a quiet neighborhood in Kentucky, those larger debates felt distant. But they were already shaping the world around me. And in ways I did not realize, they were shaping the journey I would spend the rest of my life learning to understand. For many years, I carried a simplified version of the world in my mind.

It was a version where outcomes seemed connected primarily to effort. Where neighborhoods reflected personal choices. Where differences appeared natural rather than constructed

That understanding was not unusual. It was inherited. Many people of my generation grew up with similar assumptions, shaped by limited exposure and incomplete narratives about how American communities developed. What I would later learn is that understanding history requires more than awareness of events.

It requires a willingness to reconsider the explanations we were first given. And sometimes, that process can be uncomfortable. Because it asks us to see familiar places—and familiar stories—through a different lens.

My first vivid memory of racial conflict came during the late 1960s.

The assassination of Martin Luther King Jr. in 1968 shocked the nation. I was in the fifth grade. Even children sensed the gravity of what had happened. Teachers spoke in somber tones, and television news showed demonstrations unfolding across the country.

For the first time, I began to realize that race relations in America were far more complicated than I had previously imagined. Yet the deeper meaning of those events remained distant from my everyday life.

Like many White Americans of that era, I believed racial conflict was primarily a Southern problem. It seemed to belong to another place and another community. I did not yet recognize how deeply those issues were woven into the fabric of American society—including my own hometown.

Even as a child, I could sense that something had shifted. My eyes were being opened to the reality of racial discrimination. On occasion, when my older sisters' Black male friends visited our home – some of our neighbors looked upon this with disgust.

When my father, a top official in our county, appointed the first Black man as Deputy Judge Executive, his political adversaries tried to use this decision to discredit him. Television broadcasts carried a tone that felt heavier than usual. The images on the screen—marches, protests, unrest—seemed different from the everyday news I was accustomed to seeing.

But understanding did not come easily. For many of us, those events felt distant, even as they unfolded across the country. We did not yet have the framework to connect those national moments to the local realities around us.

It would take time—and experience—before those pieces began to come together. Before I understood that the turmoil I was witnessing was not isolated. It was part of a much larger story.

Looking back now, I understand that the differences I observed as a child were shaped by forces much larger than I could comprehend at the time. The invisible lines running through Covington were not accidental. They reflected decades of housing policy, segregation, and unequal opportunity that shaped communities across America.

Clara represented one of the first lines I would eventually cross.

KEY INSIGHT

The lines that divide people are not always visible. Sometimes they are found in neighborhoods, opportunities, and assumptions we inherit without question. Understanding begins when we move beyond observation and ask why those lines exist.

Chapter 2

Friendship as a Teacher

I attended a Catholic high school with a graduating class of about seventy students. Only two students were Black.
A few others were Asian.

At the time, that level of diversity seemed normal. It reflected what I had come to expect in my environment, and I did not yet have the perspective to question it. Looking back now, I recognize how limited that exposure truly was. The world I experienced in those years was far narrower than I understood.

Yet even within that limited setting, small moments began to stretch the boundaries of my awareness.

One of the Black students in our class eventually became my roommate on our senior class trip to Washington, D.C. It was not presented as anything unusual. Two students sharing a room—that was all. And in many ways, that is exactly what it was.

We talked about school, sports, music, and our plans for the future. We joked, relaxed, and navigated the trip like any other group of teenagers. There were no grand debates or defining moments. Nothing that would have seemed remarkable at the time.

And yet, something meaningful was happening beneath the surface. For perhaps the first time, I was spending extended, unstructured time with someone whose life experience might be different from my own. Not in a classroom. Not in passing. But in the ordinary rhythm of shared space—late-night conversations, morning routines, and the small, unguarded interactions that reveal who people really are.

Those conversations were ordinary. But their impact was not. They quietly expanded my perspective.

Outside of school, I spent many of my early teen years on the swimming team at the local Boys & Girls Club and YMCA. Swimming became an important part of my life—discipline, competition, and camaraderie all came together in that environment.

Even in an urban setting, however, the swim teams I competed with were overwhelmingly White. At the time, I didn't question it. It simply reflected what I saw around me.

One exception stood out—a talented Black swimmer from the Dayton, Ohio YMCA. He was fast, disciplined, and highly respected in competition. Over time, we developed a friendship grounded in our shared commitment to the sport.

In the 1970s, swimming was still a sport with very limited Black participation. That reality made his presence all the more significant, though I did not fully grasp it at the time. What I did understand was this: he was a competitor I admired and a teammate I respected.

Our connection was built in the water through practices, meets, and the mutual understanding that comes from pushing yourself to improve. We didn't spend much time analyzing differences. We were focused on performance, goals, and the shared language of sport.

But again, something subtle was taking place. Each interaction added another layer to my understanding of people beyond the narrow boundaries I had inherited.

At about the age of sixteen, another door opened in an unexpected way. I began dating a Chinese girl. Through her, I encountered a world that felt both unfamiliar and fascinating. Her family introduced me to traditions, values, and perspectives that were different from anything I had experienced before.

Meals were not just meals—they were expressions of culture. Family interactions carried a tone and rhythm that felt distinct. Respect, communication, and expectations often reflected values I had not previously considered. At first, I was simply observing. Trying to understand. Learning what questions to ask—and sometimes realizing how much I didn't yet know.

There were moments of awkwardness, as there often are when stepping into unfamiliar cultural spaces. But there were also moments of genuine connection—shared laughter, hospitality, and a growing appreciation for the richness of traditions different from my own.

What began as a teenage relationship became something more meaningful. It became an introduction to a broader human experience.

None of these friendships instantly transformed my understanding of race or culture. There was no single moment where everything suddenly became clear. No dramatic shift in perspective that changed everything overnight.

Instead, the process was gradual. A conversation here. A shared experience there. A realization that surfaced quietly, often long after the moment had passed. Looking back, I see these experiences for what they were: Seeds. Seeds of awareness. Seeds of curiosity. Seeds of empathy.

At the time, they seemed small—almost insignificant within the larger story of my life. But over time, they began to take root.

They challenged assumptions I didn't know I had. They widened my field of vision. They prepared me—slowly and imperfectly—for deeper understanding in the years ahead. Growth, I would later learn, rarely comes all at once. More often, it begins in moments that feel entirely ordinary. And only in hindsight do we recognize just how important those moments were.

During graduate school, one of my friendships quietly reshaped how I began to see the world.

At the time, I was still in the early stages of expanding my perspective about race and culture in America. Many of my assumptions had never been seriously challenged. I had grown up in environments where most of the people around me shared similar backgrounds. Even when I encountered diversity, I often interpreted those experiences through my own limited frame of reference.

That began to change through a friendship that developed almost casually.

One of my classmates was a Black colleague who shared an interest in golf. We started playing together occasionally, sometimes on weekends and sometimes when our schedules allowed a quick round after classes.

Golf, like many sports, has a way of creating space for conversation. Long walks between shots often become opportunities to talk about work, life, and the small frustrations and joys that come with both.

At first, our conversations were much like those between either of our friends. We talked about school. We talked about sports. We talked about the uncertain paths young professionals often face as they begin building careers.

But over time, I began to notice something that had never occurred to me before. When we arrived at certain golf courses, subtle reactions sometimes followed. Nothing dramatic happened. No one refused us service. No one said anything openly offensive.

Yet occasionally, there would be a moment of hesitation when we checked in at the clubhouse. A brief pause. A quick glance between staff members. Other golfers sometimes looked in our direction before returning to their conversations. For me, those moments barely registered at first.

Golf courses had always felt like comfortable environments. I had never questioned whether I belonged there. From my perspective, we were simply two friends playing a round of golf. But gradually I began to recognize that my friend's experience might be different from my own.

One afternoon, as we walked down the fairway, he shared a story about a golf course where he had once felt unwelcome. The staff had been polite, but their body language suggested uncertainty about his presence. He told the story calmly, without anger or bitterness. For him, these kinds of moments were simply part of navigating the world.

For me, the story opened a door I had never previously walked through. Before that conversation, I had rarely considered how environments communicate belonging—or exclusion—without anyone speaking a word. Spaces send signals. Sometimes those signals are welcoming. Sometimes they are subtle reminders that someone is viewed as different.

For most of my life, I had moved through the world without needing to think about those signals. Listening to my friend's experiences made me realize that others did not always have that same luxury. That realization did not arrive as a dramatic revelation.

Instead, it developed slowly through our conversations and time spent together. Friendship has a way of expanding perspective in ways that books or lectures rarely can. When we spend time with people whose backgrounds differ from our own, we begin to see the world through their experiences.

Our conversations eventually touched on deeper subjects. Occasionally, my friend would describe moments when he felt watched in places where others moved freely. Other times, he spoke about wondering whether certain reactions from people were influenced by race. These were not stories about dramatic confrontations. They were often quiet observations. Subtle experiences. Small signals that might pass unnoticed by someone who had never needed to interpret them.

But subtle experiences repeated over time can shape how a person moves through the world.

Listening to those stories helped me begin to understand something I had never needed to think about before: the constant awareness that many minority individuals carry as they move through environments that were historically designed for someone else.

Before those conversations, I rarely considered how much effort it might require for someone to evaluate whether they would feel comfortable—or even welcome—in certain places.

For me, most environments simply felt normal. For my friend, the calculation was sometimes different. That awareness opened my eyes to a larger truth. Many of the social systems surrounding us are experienced very differently depending on where a person begins their journey.

Friendship became one of the most powerful teachers in my life. Not because my friend set out to educate me. But because relationships naturally create opportunities for understanding. The more time we spent talking and sharing experiences, the more I realized how limited my earlier perspective had been.

Exposure to different cultures and backgrounds does not automatically erase misunderstanding or bias. But relationships create opportunities to ask questions. They allow us to listen. And sometimes they reveal realities we might never have noticed on our own. That friendship became one of the early steps in a much longer journey. A journey of learning to see the world from perspectives beyond my own.

It was not the final lesson. In many ways, it was only the beginning. But it marked an important moment when curiosity began replacing assumptions. And when I started to recognize that understanding often grows not from debate or theory, but from the simple act of listening to another person's story.

That friendship did not provide me with immediate answers. Instead, it gave me something more valuable. It gave me new questions. Questions about how environments communicate belonging. Questions about how people experience the same space differently. Questions about how many things I had taken for granted simply because I had never needed to think about them. Those questions stayed with me. And over time, they became part of a larger shift. A shift from assuming to asking. From observing to listening. From seeing the world as fixed—to recognizing that perspective itself can change.

Friendship has a way of expanding perspective in ways that books or lectures rarely can. When we spend time with people whose backgrounds differ from our own, we begin to see the world through their experiences. My friendship with that colleague did exactly that.

We talked about sports, work, and life—ordinary conversations between friends. Yet occasionally our discussions touched on deeper subjects. I began to hear stories about experiences that had never occurred to me before. Moments when my friend felt watched in places where others moved freely. Moments when he wondered whether certain reactions from people were based on race. Moments when he carried a quiet awareness that he might be perceived differently in professional or social settings. These were not dramatic incidents. They were subtle. But subtle experiences repeated over time can shape a person's relationship with the world.

Listening to those stories helped me begin to understand something I had never needed to think about before: the constant awareness many minority individuals carry as they move through environments that were historically designed for someone else. It was another step in my growing awareness.

One afternoon stands out more clearly than the others. We had just finished a round of golf and were sitting outside the clubhouse. The late afternoon sun stretched long shadows across the course. It was quiet, the kind of quiet that invites conversation. I leaned back on the bench and said something I had believed most of my life.

"You know, I've always felt like if you work hard enough, things tend to work out." It felt like common sense. Something I had heard growing up. My friend didn't respond immediately. He looked out across the fairway for a moment, then turned toward me. "I get that," he said calmly. "And hard work does matter." He paused. "But it's not always the same for everyone."

I remember feeling slightly defensive, though I wasn't sure why. "What do you mean?" I asked. He leaned forward, resting his forearms on his knees. "I've worked hard my whole life," he said. "But there are times I walk into a place—and before I even say a word, I can feel people trying to figure out why I'm there." I thought about the subtle moments I had begun noticing. The glances. The pauses.

"I don't mean anyone says anything," he continued. "Most people are polite. But you can feel it." He tapped his chest lightly. "You learn to read it." I sat quietly. "For you," he said, "you just show up—and that's enough." He said it without accusation. "For me, sometimes I feel like I have to prove I belong before I've even opened my mouth." That sentence stayed with me.

One of the themes that continued throughout my life was curiosity about other cultures. Travel, friendships, and professional relationships all contributed to that curiosity. The more I encountered people from different backgrounds, the more fascinated I became by the richness of human experience. Food traditions. Family structures. Religious practices. Political systems. Languages. Each culture carried its own way of interpreting the world. And each interaction reminded me that no single perspective holds all the answers.

Exposure to diverse cultures does not automatically eliminate bias or misunderstanding. But it does create opportunities for empathy and learning. The more relationships we build across cultural lines, the more difficult it becomes to hold simplistic assumptions about entire groups of people.

That realization would later become an important foundation for my work in leadership and diversity initiatives. Not every moment of learning comes through calm reflection. Some come through misunderstandings.

One evening, a group of international students gathered for dinner in my apartment. It was more like a meeting of the United Nations. I think there were about 10 different nationalities represented. I had a Japanese roommate at the time, who had invited many of his college friends to join us.

The table included students from several different backgrounds, and the conversation moved easily from schoolwork to travel, to family traditions, to cultural differences.

At one point, the discussion turned to neighborhoods and where people felt comfortable living. Without thinking much about it, I commented. "I've always believed people should just choose the best neighborhood they can afford," I said. "That's what most families do." The words felt reasonable as I said them. But almost immediately, I sensed a shift at the table.

One of our guests, a Palestinian, looked at me, then set down his fork. "It's not always that simple," he said. His tone wasn't confrontational, but it was firm. I felt a slight defensiveness rise in me. "What do you mean?" I asked. He took a breath before responding.

"Where you can live isn't always just about what you can afford," he said. "Sometimes it's about where you're accepted. Or where you're not questioned." Another voice joined in. "Sometimes it's about where you're allowed to feel comfortable," someone said. "And sometimes," another added, "it's about whether you're even shown the options."

I remember thinking: *I didn't mean anything by that.* "I wasn't trying to make a point," I said. "I know," one of them replied gently. "That's kind of the point." That sentence landed harder than anything else. No one was attacking me. They were inviting me to see something I hadn't seen before.

Another guest nodded. "And sometimes," added a Black man, "it's about whether you even get an opportunity to consider a neighborhood." The table grew quiet.

I realized I had stepped into a conversation I didn't fully understand. "I didn't mean anything by it," I finally said what I was thinking. "I know," he replied. "That's kind of the point." There was no hostility in his voice. But there was something else. Clarity.

"You're looking at it from your experience," he continued. "And that's normal. But not everyone has had the same experience." I sat back in my chair, absorbing what he was saying.

For most of my life, I had assumed that housing decisions were primarily economic. Find a place you can afford. Move in. Build a life. But as the conversation continued, I began hearing a different perspective.

Stories about families being steered toward certain neighborhoods. Stories about subtle signals that indicated whether someone was welcome. Stories about feeling out of place—even in spaces that were technically open to everyone.

No one at the table was trying to prove a point. They were simply describing their experiences. And for the first time, I began to recognize how incomplete my own understanding had been. "I guess I've never had to think about that," I said quietly. "That's not a bad thing," one of them responded. "It just means there's more to see."

That evening stayed with me. Not because it was uncomfortable—though it was. But because it revealed something important. Understanding often begins at the moment we realize that our assumptions are not universal. That what feels normal to us may not feel the same to someone else. And that growth sometimes starts with the simple willingness to say: "I hadn't thought about it that way before." Moments like that do not always feel significant at the time. But over the years, they accumulate. And slowly, they begin to change how we see the world.

KEY INSIGHT

Friendship has the power to accomplish what debates and statistics often cannot. When we listen to another person's story, we begin to see the world through a wider lens and discover that understanding grows through relationships.

Chapter 3

The Great Equalizer

In my late teens and early adulthood, I struggled with alcohol. At first, drinking seemed like a normal part of social life. Many young people experiment with alcohol during those years. But gradually, my relationship with drinking became unhealthy.

Like many people dealing with addiction, I initially minimized the problem. I convinced myself that I could control it. That illusion eventually collapsed. When the consequences of my drinking became impossible to ignore, I found myself searching for a way forward.

That search led me to Alcoholics Anonymous. Walking into my first AA meeting was one of the most humbling experiences of my life. I did not know what to expect. I simply knew that something had to change. What I found inside those rooms surprised me.

Scene: An AA Meeting

The folding chairs formed a circle, as they always did. Coffee brewed in the corner while people filtered quietly into the smoke-filled room. Some greeted one another warmly; others sat silently as if gathering courage.

A man stood and introduced himself. His clothes were worn, and his voice shook slightly as he spoke about losing his job, his home, and his family. Around the room sat people whose lives looked very different from his. A business owner. A construction worker. A nurse. Even a nun and a priest. Yet no one judged him.

In that room, titles and status disappeared. The homeless man and the bank president had the same standing: member. That night, I realized something powerful. Beneath status, race, or profession, we are all human beings searching for dignity and redemption.

Alcoholics Anonymous introduced me to one of the most powerful lessons I have ever learned about humanity. Alcoholism does not discriminate. It affects people from every social class, every profession, every race, and every background.

When I began attending AA meetings, I found myself sitting in rooms filled with people whose lives looked nothing like mine.

Bank presidents.

Celebrities.

Construction workers.

Corporate executives.

Homeless men.

Teachers.

Laborers.

Artists.

Veterans.

Nuns.

In those rooms, the labels that society uses to rank people disappeared. Everyone carried the same identity: Member.

The homeless man sitting beside me had the same voice and the same standing as the CEO across the room. When people stand together in recovery, many of the divisions that normally separate them fade away. AA became one of the greatest classrooms of my life. It taught me humility. It taught me compassion. And it taught me something deeply important about equality.

Human dignity does not come from wealth, status, or professional achievement. It comes from the simple fact that we are human beings.

There is something profoundly disarming about sitting in a room where no one is pretending.

In most areas of life, people carry identities shaped by profession, status, and success. Those identities often define how we are seen—and how we see ourselves. But in that room, those layers fall away. What remains is something more fundamental.

Honesty.

Vulnerability.

Shared struggle.

And in that environment, it becomes much harder to maintain the illusions that often separate us. Because when people begin speaking openly about their lives, the differences that once seemed significant begin to fade. And the similarities become impossible to ignore.

Recovery is often described as being on a lifeboat. It is a powerful image—simple yet deeply revealing. A lifeboat is not a place of comfort or status. It is a place of necessity. No one boards a lifeboat because they want to. They board because they must. Because something in their life has broken apart, and survival now depends on reaching something steadier, something safer, something new.

In that lifeboat, everyone is trying to survive. Titles disappear. Backgrounds blur. The usual markers that define people—profession, income, education, social standing—lose their importance. The person sitting next to you may have lived a life completely different from your own. They may have made different choices, held different beliefs, walked different roads. But in that moment, none of that matters. What matters is that they are there. And so are you.

When people face that kind of shared struggle, they begin to see each other differently.

There is a quiet leveling that takes place. Not forced, not theoretical—but real. It comes from the recognition that everyone in that space is vulnerable. Everyone has known pain. Everyone is working to hold on. And something begins to shift.

The barriers that normally divide people—race, class, politics, background—become less important. Not because they disappear, but because something more urgent takes their place. Survival. Connection. Hope. What matters is helping one another stay afloat.

In Alcoholics Anonymous meetings, I saw individuals from every background imaginable working together toward a common goal. The rooms were filled with people whose lives, on the surface, might never have intersected.

A business executive might sit beside a laborer.
A college professor might listen to someone who never finished high school. A young person just beginning their journey might speak after someone with decades of life experience.

And yet, in those moments, they were not separated by those differences. They were united by a shared understanding. People who might never have spoken to each other in ordinary circumstances were sharing deeply personal stories—stories they may have never told even their closest friends. There was a level of honesty in those rooms that was both disarming and inspiring. No pretense.
No performance. No need to impress. Just truth.

They listened to each other with empathy and understanding. Not the kind of listening that waits for a turn to speak, but the kind that seeks to understand. The kind that says, *I hear you. I've been there. You're not alone.*

They celebrated one another's progress—sometimes in small ways that might go unnoticed elsewhere. A single day of sobriety. A difficult conversation handled with grace. A moment of choosing a different path. These were victories. And they mattered.

They also supported each other through setbacks. Because setbacks are part of the journey. No one in the lifeboat pretends otherwise. When someone stumbles, the response is not judgment—it is encouragement. It is a hand extended, not a finger pointed.

"Get back in," the lifeboat seems to say.
"We're still here."

That environment taught me a profound lesson. The more we see each other as fellow travelers rather than competitors, the more compassion we develop.

It is easy, in everyday life, to fall into patterns of comparison. To measure success, to draw distinctions, to create quiet hierarchies that place people above or below one another. These habits are often so ingrained that we barely notice them.

But the lifeboat challenges that way of thinking. In the lifeboat, there is no "above" or "below." There is only "with." With each other. Alongside one another. Moving forward together.

And when you begin to see people that way—not as competitors for space or recognition, but as companions in a shared journey—something changes within you. You become more patient. More understanding. More willing to listen. More willing to help. The lifeboat, in that sense, becomes more than a place of survival. It becomes a place of transformation.

Because once you have experienced that kind of connection—once you have seen what it looks like when people set aside their differences and simply care for one another—it is difficult to return to seeing the world the same way. You begin to notice opportunities to extend that same spirit beyond the lifeboat. In your workplace. In your community. In your everyday interactions.

You begin to ask different questions.

What if we approached one another with curiosity instead of judgment? What if we listened before we responded?

What if we recognized that everyone we encounter is carrying something we cannot see? The lifeboat does not eliminate differences. But it reframes them.

It reminds us that beneath those differences lies something we all share—a need for understanding, a desire for dignity, and a hope for something better. And perhaps that is the deeper lesson. We are all, in one way or another, in the same boat. And we all do better when we help each other stay afloat.

The pop group, The Hollies, recorded a song several years ago titled "He Ain't Heavy, He's My Brother," which could serve as the theme song for the AA program. One of the verses goes like this – "The road is long, with many a winding turn, that leads us to who knows where? Who knows where? But, I'm strong enough to carry him. He ain't heavy – he's my brother.

Over the years, my experience in AA has reshaped how I viewed the world. Recovery meetings became one of the most diverse communities I had ever encountered. People from every race, religion, profession, and social class gathered together for the same purpose: to live healthier lives.

Those rooms reinforced something I had begun learning through other experiences. Our differences may be visible on the surface. But our struggles, hopes, and fears are remarkably similar. When we strip away the layers of status and identity that society attaches to us, we begin to recognize the shared humanity underneath. That realization would later influence my leadership philosophy and my commitment to expanding diversity in the organizations I served.

Over the course of over 44 years of sobriety, I have sponsored many men as they begin the AA journey. All of my efforts have been successful – since I am still sober today. My purpose is to carry the message and not the alcoholic. God is responsible for getting these men sober – not me. It's heartbreaking to learn that so many who find their way to AA stray from the path. Yet, over the years, I have seen countless lives that were once shattered become whole again.

Families that were broken – have become rekindled. Jobs lost and new ones found. Those who were once hopeless becoming hope-filled. And new growth from lives that were previously barren. I've seen how AA has brought about transformations in people when they come to know and experience a loving God. For many, this is the turning point in their recovery.

As an AA sponsor, I have had the opportunity to experience this miraculous process of humanity. With each day, it becomes clearer. God does for us what we could not do for ourselves – if we let him.

KEY INSIGHT

In recovery, titles, wealth, race, and status fade into the background. Human dignity remains. The lessons learned in the lifeboat remind us that our shared humanity is far greater than our differences.

Chapter 4

Leadership that Reflected the Community

When my career brought me to Newport News, Virginia, I encountered something that challenged many of my assumptions about leadership and diversity.

Virginia, like much of the American South, carries a complicated and painful history when it comes to race. As a former slave state and part of the Confederacy, the legacy of slavery and segregation has long shaped its social and political landscape.

Yet the professional community I entered in Newport News offered a very different picture of what leadership could look like. I was serving as Executive Vice President of the regional Realtor Association. From the beginning, I noticed something unusual about the leadership structure of the organization. Black and White leaders worked side by side.

Board members shared authority and influence across racial lines. Leadership meetings reflected a level of mutual respect and collaboration that I had not often seen in other organizations. In many places, diversity was discussed as an abstract goal. In Newport News, it was simply the way the organization operated.

At the time, I did not fully appreciate how rare that environment actually was. But over the years, I came to realize that I was witnessing a model of leadership that many institutions across the country were still struggling to achieve. At first, I did not fully recognize what I was seeing. The collaboration felt natural. The diversity felt unremarkable. It simply appeared to be how the organization functioned.

But over time, I began to understand that what felt normal in that environment was actually uncommon in many others. And that realization carried an important implication. If inclusive leadership could function effectively here, it was not an abstract ideal. It was a practical reality. One that could be built. One that could be sustained.

And one that could be replicated—if organizations were willing to be intentional about it. As the leader of the organization in Virginia, I personally made intentional efforts to fill open positions on my staff with Black employees.

Newport News was more than just a step in my professional career. It provided a mosaic of how intentional diversity can build stronger organizations and a more harmonious community. One of the reasons the Realtor Association functioned so effectively was that its leadership structure mirrored the community it served.

The Virginia Peninsula region was home to a diverse population—racially, economically, and culturally—and that diversity was not just acknowledged within the organization. It was visible. It was present in leadership meetings, committee discussions, and decision-making processes. That mattered.

When leadership teams include individuals with different perspectives and lived experiences, conversations change. They become more layered. More honest. More grounded in reality. Decisions become more thoughtful. Blind spots become easier to recognize. And organizations become better equipped to serve the communities around them.

I saw this play out in ways that went far beyond policy discussions or strategic planning sessions. It showed up in how leaders listened to one another. It showed up in the questions that were asked—and just as importantly, in the assumptions that were challenged. This was not a theoretical concept. I saw it happening in real time.

In meetings, Black leaders and White leaders brought different life experiences to the table. Those differences were not sources of division—they were sources of strength. They added depth to conversations about housing access, community development, and professional opportunity within the industry.

There were moments when perspectives didn't immediately align. But instead of shutting down dialogue, those moments often opened the door to better understanding. People leaned in. They asked questions. They reconsidered their positions. And in doing so, the organization grew stronger.

What I witnessed during those years left a deep impression on me—not just as an executive, but as a person still learning how to lead. It challenged me to listen more carefully. To be more aware of my own assumptions. To recognize that my perspective, while shaped by my experiences, was not the only one that mattered.

Over time, I began to understand that diversity within leadership is not simply about representation for its own sake. It is about perspective. It is about awareness. It is about the ability to see what would otherwise go unseen. It is about strengthening leadership itself. Not just the leadership of others—
but my own.

During my time in Virginia, several historic developments reinforced the importance of inclusive leadership in ways that felt both immediate and deeply meaningful.

One of the most significant was the election of Doug Wilder (1990) as the first Black governor in the United States. For many people across the country, Wilder's election represented a milestone in American political history—a moment that signaled progress at the highest levels of leadership. For those of us living and working in Virginia at the time, it felt even more personal.

It felt like a reflection of something that had been quietly building within communities across the state for years—progress that didn't always make headlines, but was real nonetheless. Progress shaped by relationships, by conversations, and by individuals stepping into roles that had not always been accessible to them.

Around that same period, our city elected a Black woman as mayor. Again, this was more than a symbolic moment. It was a visible and tangible sign that leadership opportunities were expanding in ways that reflected the communities themselves.

These were not isolated events. They were part of a broader pattern—one that suggested that change, while often gradual, was possible.

Within the Realtor Association, we experienced our own moment of significance. A respected Black leader from our region was on track to become president of the National Association of Realtors. It was a moment that carried tremendous meaning, not only for him personally, but for the organization and the profession as a whole.

Tragically, he passed away before that milestone could be realized. Even so, his leadership and the path he had helped create did not disappear. If anything, it reinforced how important it was for opportunities to continue expanding—for others to step forward, and for the organization to remain committed to inclusive leadership.

These developments created a growing sense that meaningful change was not only possible—it was already underway. For me, these moments were not just historical markers. They were part of a broader learning process. They reinforced something I had begun to understand through both observation and personal experience: Leadership becomes stronger when it reflects the diversity of the people it serves.

Not because it checks a box. Not because it meets an expectation. But because it brings together the perspectives necessary to lead more effectively in a complex and evolving world. And once you see that clearly, you begin to understand that inclusive leadership is not an aspiration. It is a necessity.

The years I spent in Virginia shaped my understanding of leadership in ways that have stayed with me ever since. At the time, I didn't fully realize how much I was learning. I was focused on doing my job, supporting the organization, and navigating the day-to-day challenges that come with leadership roles. But looking back, those years were formative.

Watching diverse leadership teams collaborate effectively changed how I thought about organizations—not in theory, but in practice. I saw firsthand how different perspectives could elevate conversations, challenge assumptions, and ultimately lead to better decisions.

It also caused me to reconsider something I had heard often throughout my career. Many people view diversity initiatives primarily as efforts to correct historical injustice. And while that goal is both real and important, my experience in Virginia revealed something equally significant—something that is often overlooked. Diversity strengthens decision-making.

When leadership teams include individuals with different lived experiences, they are better equipped to anticipate challenges before they arise. They are more likely to ask the questions that others might not think to ask. They are better able to recognize how decisions will affect different segments of the community.

In short, they lead more effectively. I saw this in discussions about housing access, where perspectives shaped by personal experience influenced how issues were framed. I saw it in conversations about community development, where understanding local realities made strategies more grounded and practical. I saw it in professional development efforts, where inclusion created broader pathways for growth.

These were not abstract benefits. They were tangible. They were measurable. And they made a difference.

By contrast, I also began to understand the limitations of homogeneous leadership teams. Even when well-intentioned, those teams often operate within a shared set of assumptions. They may not realize what they are missing—because, from their vantage point, nothing appears to be missing. Blind spots remain hidden. Important questions go unasked. And opportunities for better outcomes can be overlooked.

This realization didn't come all at once. It developed gradually, shaped by observation, by experience, and by a growing willingness on my part to listen more carefully and reflect more honestly.

The Virginia Peninsula community provided a living example of what inclusive leadership could look like when it is embraced not as an obligation, but as a strength. It showed me that leadership is not just about directing or managing. It is about understanding. It is about perspective. It is about creating space for voices that might otherwise go unheard. And perhaps most importantly, it is about being willing to learn—even when that learning challenges your own assumptions.

Years later, when I returned to the Midwest, those lessons did not stay behind. They came with me. They influenced how I approached leadership decisions. How I built teams. How I listened. And how I understood the responsibility that comes with leading in communities that are, in many ways, both similar to and different from those I had known before.

I didn't always get it right. But I approached those opportunities with a clearer understanding than I had before—an understanding shaped by the experiences, relationships, and lessons that took root during my time in Virginia. Lessons that stayed with me. Lessons that would continue to shape the way I led. And lessons that, in many ways, were still unfolding.

KEY INSIGHT

Leadership is strongest when it reflects the people it serves. Diverse perspectives do not weaken organizations—they strengthen them by expanding understanding, improving decisions, and broadening opportunities.

Chapter 5

Building Inclusive Organizations

After leaving Virginia, my career eventually brought me back to the Midwest. I stepped into leadership roles with the Home Builders Associations of Northern Kentucky and Greater Cincinnati—organizations with long histories, strong reputations, and deep roots within the housing industry.

These were organizations I respected. They had been built over decades by committed professionals who cared deeply about their work, their members, and the communities they served. But as I settled into those roles, I began to notice something familiar. And something different.

Like many professional associations connected to construction and development, these organizations were overwhelmingly White—particularly at the leadership level. That reality was not unusual.

The housing industry, especially in leadership roles, had historically lacked diversity. For years, that had simply been accepted as part of the landscape—rarely questioned, and even more rarely addressed in any meaningful way.

But the communities these organizations served were not static. They were changing. Neighborhoods were becoming more diverse. New voices were emerging. Different perspectives were shaping how people thought about housing, access, and opportunity. And the contrast between those two realities became increasingly difficult to ignore.

On one side, organizations with long-standing leadership structures that looked much as they always had.
On the other hand, communities that were evolving in ways that those structures did not yet fully reflect.

That contrast raised an important question: How could organizations effectively serve communities that were changing—if their leadership remained the same? It was not a question of criticism. It was a question of alignment. And for me, it was not an abstract idea.

It was a question shaped by what I had seen in Virginia—by the understanding that leadership becomes stronger when it reflects the diversity of the people it serves. I began to realize that the lessons I had learned there were not meant to stay there. They were meant to be applied.

At first, that realization came with a degree of uncertainty. These organizations had established cultures, traditions, and ways of operating that had served them well for many years. Any effort to introduce new ideas—especially around leadership and inclusion—needed to be approached thoughtfully and with respect.

Change, I had learned, is rarely effective when it is forced. It is far more effective when it is understood. So the work began not with sweeping changes, but with conversations.

Conversations about who was at the table—and who was not.
Conversations about how decisions were being made—and whose perspectives were shaping those decisions.
Conversations about what it would mean to more fully reflect the communities the organizations were intended to serve.

Some of those conversations were easy. Others were not. But they were necessary. Over time, those discussions began to take shape in the form of early initiatives—small at first, but intentional. Efforts to broaden participation. Efforts to identify and encourage emerging leaders from different backgrounds. Efforts to create pathways into leadership that had not always been visible or accessible.

These were not dramatic shifts. They were deliberate steps. Steps rooted in a simple belief:

That organizations are strongest when they are connected to the full breadth of the communities they represent. I didn't approach this work with all the answers. But I did approach it with a clearer sense of direction—one shaped by experience, by observation, and by a growing understanding of what effective leadership requires.

The lessons from Virginia had come with me. And now, they were beginning to take form in a new place—in familiar communities, within established organizations, and in a leadership journey that was continuing to evolve.

Introducing diversity initiatives within established organizations is rarely easy. Long-standing institutions develop traditions, habits, and unspoken norms over time. Those patterns often provide stability and continuity—but they can also make change feel disruptive, even when that change is necessary.

I understood that going in. What I didn't fully appreciate at first was how differently people would respond to the conversation. Some members welcomed it.

They recognized that the future of the housing industry would depend on reaching broader communities—communities that were growing, evolving, and increasingly shaping the direction of the marketplace itself. To them, expanding participation wasn't just the right thing to do—it was a practical necessity. But not everyone saw it that way. Others were skeptical.

Some questioned whether diversity initiatives were necessary at all. From their perspective, the organizations had functioned effectively for years. Membership was strong. Relationships were established. The systems in place had produced results. So why change? Others expressed a different concern—one that was often less direct, but just as real.

They worried that a focus on inclusion might somehow diminish opportunities for existing members. That expanding the circle might mean taking something away from those who had long been part of it. These concerns were not always expressed openly.

They surfaced in conversations on the margins. In questions that hinted at deeper uncertainty. In pauses, in hesitation, in the tone of discussions that didn't always make their way into official minutes. But they were present. And ignoring them would not have made them disappear.

Leadership, I came to understand, requires navigating these tensions with care. It requires listening—not just to what is said, but to what is felt. It requires patience, because meaningful change rarely happens quickly. And it requires persistence, because progress can stall if leaders lose focus or resolve.

We made a conscious decision early on about how to frame the conversation. Rather than positioning diversity solely as a moral obligation, we spoke about it in terms of effectiveness.

We asked questions that connected inclusion to the future of the industry: How do we reach communities that are not currently engaged? How do we build trust where relationships have not yet been established? How do we ensure that the next generation of leaders reflects the full range of people who will shape the housing market?

These were not abstract questions. They were business questions. Leadership questions. Strategic questions. And over time, that framing began to shift the conversation. Not for everyone. Not all at once. But gradually. People began to see that this was not about replacing one group with another.

It was about expanding the table. Creating more opportunity—not less. Building a stronger organization—not a different one disconnected from its past. Still, the process was not linear. Change rarely announces itself with clarity. More often, it begins with uncertainty. Questions surface before answers. Concerns emerge before consensus. And leaders find themselves navigating conversations where the outcome is not yet clear.

In those moments, the role of leadership is not to eliminate discomfort. It is to guide people through it. To create space for

honest dialogue—even when that dialogue is difficult.
To acknowledge concerns without allowing them to stall progress.
To keep the organization focused not only on what it has been, but on what it is becoming. There were times when progress felt slow. Times when it would have been easier to step back, to avoid the tension, to let the conversation fade.

But leadership does not move forward by avoiding difficulty. It moves forward by engaging it. By staying present in the conversation. By continuing to listen. By reinforcing the purpose behind the effort—even when the path forward is still taking shape.

Looking back, those early steps were not defined by sweeping changes or immediate breakthroughs. They were defined by something quieter. A willingness to begin. A willingness to ask questions that had not always been asked. A willingness to consider perspectives that had not always been heard. A willingness to move, even without complete certainty. And in many ways, that is where meaningful change always starts.

One of the most important steps we took was establishing the first Diversity Committee within the Home Builders Association of Greater Cincinnati. The committee had a clear mission: to recruit minority members and create pathways for leadership development. Specifically, we sought to engage: Black professionals, Women, Latino entrepreneurs, and Asian business leaders.

Our goal was not simply to increase membership numbers. We wanted to cultivate future leaders who could contribute to the long-term vitality of the organization.

The committee began developing several initiatives. Minority trades training programs were established to help individuals enter the construction workforce. Educational scholarships were created to support students interested in careers related to building and development. Community outreach efforts expanded partnerships with organizations that served diverse populations. Each of these programs represented a step toward building a more inclusive industry.

When the idea of creating a Diversity Committee was introduced, the room fell quiet. Some members supported the proposal immediately. Others questioned why it was necessary.

One longtime member asked, "Why do we need this?" It was a fair question, but it revealed how easily organizations overlook the quiet barriers that shape who participates and who leads.

We talked about the future of the construction industry. We talked about leadership pipelines and communities we served. By the end of the discussion, the proposal passed.

Looking back, that vote represented more than a new committee. It was the moment the organization chose to widen its vision of what it wanted to be. Despite the progress we were making, not everyone embraced the initiative.

Some members questioned the purpose of the Diversity Committee. They wondered whether it was necessary, or whether it might pull the organization away from what they believed were its core responsibilities. Others felt strongly that the association should remain focused on traditional industry concerns—advocacy, regulation, and business development—rather than engaging in what they perceived as broader social issues.

These perspectives were not expressed with hostility as much as with caution. Many of the individuals raising these concerns had spent years, even decades, contributing to the organization's success. Their questions came from a place of wanting to protect what they valued.

Still, the tension was real. There is a natural friction that emerges whenever institutions begin to evolve. People become accustomed to how things have always been done. They develop trust in familiar systems and relationships. When new ideas are introduced—especially ideas that challenge long-standing patterns—it can feel less like progress and more like disruption. In those moments, resistance often follows.

Over time, I came to understand that resistance is not always opposition. More often, it is uncertainty. It is a reflection of unanswered questions, unspoken concerns, or a lack of clarity about what change will actually look like in practice. That understanding shaped how I approached leadership during this period.

Leadership in moments of change requires a careful balance of patience and conviction. Patience means taking the time to listen—without defensiveness—to the concerns being raised. It means acknowledging that people need space to process new ideas. It requires a willingness to engage in conversations that may be uncomfortable but are necessary for trust to develop.

Conviction, however, is equally important. Conviction is what keeps the work moving forward. It is the clarity of purpose that allows a leader to say, "This matters," even when consensus has not yet been reached. Without conviction, initiatives lose direction. With it, they gain momentum. We made a conscious effort to hold both.

We listened carefully to feedback. We invited dialogue. We encouraged members to ask questions and to express their concerns openly. At the same time, we remained clear about why the work was important. The purpose of our efforts was not to divide the organization. It was to strengthen it.

We emphasized that building a more inclusive organization was not a departure from the mission—it was an investment in its future. An organization that reflects a wider range of perspectives is better equipped to adapt, to innovate, and to serve an increasingly diverse marketplace.

But words alone were not enough to shift perceptions. What ultimately began to change attitudes was experience. As new programs were introduced, members had the opportunity to see the initiative in action. Minority trades training programs began creating pathways into the workforce. Scholarship recipients brought new energy and perspective into the industry. Community partnerships opened doors to relationships that had not previously existed. These were not abstract ideas. They were tangible outcomes. Gradually, skepticism began to soften.

Members who had initially questioned the initiative started to recognize its value—not as a political statement, but as a practical strategy for growth and sustainability. Conversations became less about whether the work should be done and more about how it could be done effectively. The shift was subtle.

There was no single turning point, no moment when resistance disappeared entirely. Instead, attitudes evolved over time, shaped by repeated exposure to positive results and consistent messaging about purpose. This experience reinforced something I have come to believe deeply: Change rarely happens overnight. It unfolds through a series of small steps—conversations, decisions, and actions that, taken together, begin to move an organization in a new direction.

Persistence is what makes that movement possible. Persistence is not about forcing change. It is about sustaining effort. It is about showing up consistently, even when progress feels slow. It is about maintaining focus when enthusiasm fluctuates and continuing the work when results are not immediately visible.

In many ways, persistence becomes the bridge between vision and reality. Looking back, I realize that the resistance we encountered was not a sign that the initiative was misguided. It was a sign that it mattered. It meant that we were engaging with ideas that challenged assumptions and invited growth. It meant that the organization was being asked to think differently about its role and its future.

And in the end, it was persistence—steady, patient, and grounded in purpose—that allowed those ideas to take root. Over time, expectations began to shift.

What once felt new and uncertain gradually became part of the organization's identity. The work of inclusion moved from the margins toward the center. And what began as an initiative became, in many respects, a shared commitment. That is the nature of meaningful change. It begins with vision, encounters resistance, and is sustained through persistence.

Years after the Diversity Committee began its work, the Home Builders Association of Greater Cincinnati elected its first Black president in 2025.

For many people outside the organization, the moment may have appeared routine—another leadership transition, another year, another name added to a long list of past presidents. But for those of us who understood the organization's history, it was anything but routine. It was a milestone.

For decades, leadership positions within the association had been occupied almost exclusively by White members. That reality had not always been questioned. It had simply reflected the patterns and pathways that had existed within the industry for generations.

Change, when it came, did not happen suddenly. It was the result of years of effort—years of conversations, of building awareness, of encouraging broader participation, and of creating pathways that had not always been visible or accessible.

The work of the Diversity Committee had been part of that process. It had not produced immediate transformation. It had not changed everything at once. But it had created movement. It had opened doors. It had expanded conversations. It had helped people begin to see the organization not only as it had been, but as it could become. And over time, those incremental changes began to accumulate. New voices became more present. New leaders began to emerge. New perspectives started to shape the direction of the organization.

Until eventually, a moment arrived that reflected something larger than any single election. The election of the first Black president signaled that the organization was evolving.

It demonstrated that leadership opportunities were expanding—not as a symbolic gesture, but as a reflection of real progress. It showed that the pathways into leadership were becoming more inclusive, and that the organization was beginning to more fully reflect the diversity of the community it served.

For me, that moment carried a meaning that went beyond the event itself. It connected directly back to the lessons I had learned years earlier in Virginia—the understanding that leadership becomes stronger when it reflects the people it serves.

What I had seen there in principle, I was now seeing take shape in practice. And that realization made the moment even more significant. I thought about the early conversations. The questions. The uncertainty. The skepticism that had, at times, made progress feel slow.

I thought about the individuals who had stepped forward—those who had been willing to participate, to lead, and to help move the organization in a new direction. And I thought about how change, when it is sustained over time, often becomes visible in moments like this. Not as a sudden breakthrough— but as the result of consistent, intentional effort.

For me personally, that moment remains one of the proudest accomplishments of my professional career. Not because of any individual credit. In fact, it is meaningful precisely because it was not about any one person. It was about a collective willingness to grow. A willingness to examine long-standing patterns. A willingness to expand opportunity. A willingness to build an organization that could better serve a changing community.

Moments like that do not happen by accident. They happen because people choose to move forward—sometimes slowly, sometimes imperfectly—but with a shared sense of purpose.

And when they do, the results speak for themselves. Not just in who is elected, but in what that election represents.

KEY INSIGHT

Meaningful inclusion rarely begins with sweeping change. It starts with intentional conversations, thoughtful leadership, and a willingness to create opportunities for voices that have not always been heard.

Chapter 6

Faith, Family, and Calling

One of the greatest responsibilities my wife, Donna Dressman, and I shared was raising our son and two daughters in a way that emphasized character over appearance.

We knew early on that values are not simply taught—they are absorbed. Children learn far more from what they observe than from what they are told. They watch how we treat others. They notice who we welcome into our lives. They pay attention to what we prioritize, even when we don't realize they are paying attention at all.

Because of that, we understood that the values we hoped to instill would be shaped not only by conversations at the dinner table, but also by the environments we chose and the relationships we encouraged. Where we lived mattered. Who our children interacted with mattered. What they experienced on a daily basis mattered.

When our family moved to a more diverse community in Cincinnati, it created new opportunities for those experiences to take shape in natural and meaningful ways. Our daughters began attending schools where their classmates came from a wide range of racial, cultural, and socioeconomic backgrounds. It wasn't something that needed to be explained or emphasized—it was simply the reality of their everyday lives.

By that time, our son had already entered college, beginning his own journey into a broader and more independent world. For our daughters, friendships formed quickly—and those friendships reflected the diversity around them. They had friends who were Black. Friends who were Asian. Friends whose family traditions, languages, and life experiences were different from our own. And yet, to them, those differences were not barriers.

They were simply part of who their friends were. Watching those friendships develop reinforced something I had come to believe more deeply over time: Children rarely begin with prejudice. They are open. They are curious. They are accepting in ways that adults often have to relearn.

Attitudes about difference are shaped over time—by what children hear, what they see, and what is reinforced around them. That understanding shaped how we approached parenting.

Our goal was not to deliver perfect lessons or scripted conversations. It was something simpler—and, in many ways, more important. We wanted our children to see people as individuals rather than categories.

To recognize that every person has a story. That every person deserves to be treated with respect. And that character is revealed not by appearance, but by how someone lives, treats others, and responds to challenges.

We talked about kindness—not as an abstract idea, but as something lived out in everyday interactions. We emphasized honesty—even when it was difficult. Responsibility—even when no one was watching. Empathy—even when understanding required effort. And just as importantly, we tried to model those values in our own lives.

Because children notice consistency. They notice when actions align with words—and when they don't. Over time, these lessons became part of the culture of our family. Not because they were enforced, but because they were lived. They showed up in the friendships our children chose. In the way they spoke about others. In the respect they demonstrated in situations where differences could have created distance, but instead created understanding.

As a parent, there are few things more meaningful than watching your children navigate the world with a sense of awareness and compassion. It doesn't happen all at once. And it doesn't happen perfectly. But it happens through moments—through conversations, through experiences, and through the quiet, consistent reinforcement of what truly matters.

Looking back, I realize that the lessons we hoped to teach our children were not separate from the lessons I was learning in my professional life. They were connected.

The same principles that strengthen leadership—listening, understanding, valuing different perspectives—are the ones that shape how we raise our children. And in that sense, the work of building stronger organizations and the work of building a strong family are not all that different.

Both require intention. Both require example. And both require a belief that people should be seen—not for how they appear—but for who they are.

KEY INSIGHT

Progress often occurs one conversation, one relationship, and one decision at a time. Lasting change is built through consistent actions rather than dramatic gestures.

Chapter 7

Finding Community at Crossroads

In 2010, Donna, my wife, and I began attending Crossroads Church in Cincinnati. What began as a search for spiritual growth soon became something more.

Like many people, we initially came looking for connection through worship, teaching, and a deeper understanding of faith. But over time, we discovered that the most meaningful growth often happened outside of the main service—through relationships, through shared experiences, and through opportunities to serve alongside others.

Through volunteer work, small groups, and community outreach, we began building relationships with people from many different backgrounds.

Some were long-time residents of the area. Others were new to the city. Some came from professional backgrounds similar to ours. Others had life experiences that were very different. What brought us together was not similarity. It was a shared purpose.

Church communities, at their best, have the ability to bring together individuals who might not otherwise cross paths. People who, in the normal rhythms of life, might remain in separate circles—defined by profession, neighborhood, or social networks—find themselves working side by side.

At Crossroads, we encountered people whose experiences differed significantly from our own. People from different professions. Different cultural backgrounds. Different stages of life. Different personal journeys—some marked by stability, others by challenge or transition. And yet, in that setting, those differences did not create distance. They created opportunities. Opportunity to listen. Opportunity to learn. Opportunity to see the world through a lens that was not our own. Working alongside others in volunteer projects and ministry teams reinforced something I had been learning in other areas of my life:

Shared purpose has a way of bridging differences that might otherwise feel significant. When people come together around a common goal—serving others, supporting a community, or simply walking alongside one another in faith—the categories that often separate us begin to lose their hold. Conversations become more personal. Understanding becomes more natural. And relationships begin to form in ways that are grounded in something deeper than surface-level differences.

Faith communities, when functioning well, create space for this kind of connection. They create environments where people are seen not as representatives of groups, but as individuals—each with their own story, their own challenges, and their own strengths. They remind us that while our experiences may differ, our humanity is shared.

For me, those experiences at Crossroads continued to expand my understanding of what it means to be part of a diverse community. Not a community defined by uniformity—but one strengthened by difference. It reinforced the idea that diversity, when paired with shared values, does not divide.

It deepens. It strengthens relationships. It broadens perspective. And it creates a sense of connection that is rooted not in sameness, but in understanding.

Over time, the relationships we formed through the church became an important part of our lives. They were not always easy. They did not always come naturally. But they were meaningful.

And they reminded me of something that had been unfolding across different chapters of my life: Whether in professional organizations, neighborhoods, or faith communities, the principles are often the same.

When people are willing to come together, to listen, and to engage with one another beyond surface-level differences, something important begins to happen. Barriers begin to soften. Assumptions begin to fade. And community begins to take shape. Not perfectly. Not all at once. But steadily—through relationships, through shared experiences, and through a willingness to see one another more clearly.

As my professional career in the housing industry began to wind down, another opportunity began to take shape—one that had been quietly present in my life for many years. For as long as I could remember, I had carried an ambition to pursue a doctorate.

It wasn't something I spoke about often. It didn't feel urgent in the midst of building a career, raising a family, and taking on leadership responsibilities. Like many long-term aspirations, it remained in the background—something I hoped to return to "someday."

For a long time, that someday never quite arrived. There were always responsibilities that required attention. Always priorities that felt more immediate. Always reasons to wait. But over time, something began to shift.

As one chapter of my professional life started to slow, space began to open for reflection. And with that reflection came a renewed sense that the goal I had carried for so long was still there—unfinished, but not forgotten. Eventually, the timing felt right.

I enrolled at Xavier University and began working toward a Doctor of Education degree in leadership studies. From the beginning, I knew the experience would be demanding.

What I did not fully anticipate was just how transformative it would become. Returning to graduate study later in life requires a certain level of humility. You enter an environment where expectations are high, where the pace is rigorous, and where the standards for thinking, writing, and research are exacting. There is no shortcut.

You are required to engage deeply with ideas. To analyze, not just observe. To question, not just accept. And perhaps most challenging of all, you are asked to examine your own assumptions—many of which have been shaped over decades of personal and professional experience. At times, that process was uncomfortable.

There were moments when I had to step back and reconsider perspectives I had once taken for granted. Moments when the academic framework required me to look at familiar experiences through a more critical and structured lens. But those moments were also where the greatest growth occurred.

The discipline of research brought a new level of clarity to ideas I had encountered throughout my career. Concepts that had once been intuitive became more defined. Observations that had been based on experience were now supported—and sometimes challenged—by data and analysis.

The work was demanding. Balancing coursework, research, and writing with the rhythms of everyday life required focus and persistence. There were long hours, deadlines, and the constant pressure to maintain momentum. But there was also a deep sense of purpose.

This was not simply an academic exercise. It was an opportunity to connect years of lived experience with structured inquiry—to bring together what I had seen in practice with what could be understood through research.

When it came time to select a dissertation topic, the choice felt clear. I focused on a subject that had been central to much of my professional journey:

Perceived Barriers and Reported Strategies for Increasing Diversity on the Board of Directors of Builder Associations.

The topic was not abstract. It was rooted in real challenges—challenges I had encountered firsthand in the organizations I had served. As I conducted interviews, reviewed literature, and analyzed findings, a consistent pattern began to emerge.

Leadership diversity does not occur automatically. It does not happen simply because an organization expresses a desire for change. It requires intentional effort.

Organizations must be willing to examine their structures—how leadership pathways are defined, how candidates are identified, and how opportunities are communicated. They must look closely at recruitment practices. At mentorship and sponsorship opportunities. At the informal networks that often shape who is invited into leadership roles—and who is not.

In many cases, the barriers were not the result of explicit exclusion. They were the result of systems that had developed over time—systems that, while familiar and functional for some, did not provide equal access for all. Understanding those dynamics was critical. Because once they are recognized, they can be addressed.

The research confirmed much of what I had observed over the years. But it also gave those observations greater depth and credibility. It provided a framework for understanding not just *that* challenges existed, but *why* they persisted—and *how* they might be overcome.

Completing the dissertation was a five-year journey. There were moments of progress. Moments of frustration. Moments when the finish line felt distant. But there was also a steady commitment to continue—to keep writing, to keep refining, to keep moving forward. And when the work was finally complete, it represented more than the achievement of a degree.

It represented the fulfillment of a long-held goal. One that had waited patiently through the demands of career and family. One that required persistence, discipline, and a willingness to begin again at a stage of life when many might choose not to.

Looking back, the experience stands as one of the most challenging—and most fulfilling—accomplishments of my life. Not only for what it required.

But for what it revealed. That growth does not have an expiration date. That learning can begin again at any point. And that the goals we carry quietly over time often remain with us for a reason. Waiting—not to be forgotten—but to be realized.

After completing my doctorate, another unexpected chapter of my life began. I joined the faculty at the University of Cincinnati as an Assistant Professor of Management.

It was a transition I had not fully anticipated earlier in my career. For years, my work had been rooted in the day-to-day realities of industry leadership—making decisions, building teams, navigating challenges, and working alongside professionals committed to their craft.

Now, I found myself in a different environment. A classroom. A place not defined by immediate outcomes, but by preparation.
Not by quarterly results, but by long-term development.
Not by leading organizations directly, but by helping shape those who would lead them in the future.

The shift required adjustment. But it also felt like a natural extension of everything I had experienced. Transitioning from industry leadership into academia provided a new platform—one where I could reflect on the lessons I had learned and share them in a way that might influence the next generation of leaders.

Each semester, I work with senior business students who are preparing to enter leadership roles in organizations across the country. They arrive with energy, ambition, and a desire to succeed. Many are highly capable. Many are confident. And many are stepping into professional environments that will challenge them in ways they have not yet fully encountered.

Among those challenges are questions surrounding diversity, equity, and inclusion—issues that, for some students, are being considered for the first time in a professional context. That reality creates both an opportunity and a responsibility.

My goal as an educator is not simply to present theories of leadership. There is value in theory. It provides structure and language. It helps students understand established frameworks and models.

But leadership is not learned through theory alone. It is developed through reflection, through application, and through a willingness to engage with complex and sometimes uncomfortable realities.

In the classroom, I encourage students to think critically about what it means to lead. Not just how to lead effectively—but how to lead responsibly. We discuss influence—not as a tool for personal advancement, but as a responsibility that affects others. We examine decision-making—not only in terms of outcomes, but in terms of impact. And we explore what it means to build organizations where individuals are not only present, but also able to contribute fully.

Leadership, at its core, is about stewardship. It's sometimes referred to as servant leadership. It is about recognizing that positions of authority come with an obligation to serve others—not simply to direct them. It requires the ability to see people as individuals. To recognize their dignity. And to create environments where their talents, perspectives, and experiences are valued.

Those conversations are not always easy. Students bring different perspectives into the classroom. Different experiences. Different levels of exposure to the topics we discuss. But that diversity of thought becomes part of the learning process. Because leadership does not take place in uniform environments. It takes place in complexity.

The classroom also provides opportunities to extend learning beyond textbooks and lectures. One of the most meaningful aspects of my role is bringing in guest speakers—leaders from a variety of backgrounds who are willing to share their experiences openly and honestly.

Many of these individuals come from underrepresented communities. They speak candidly about the challenges they have faced, the barriers they have navigated, and the strategies they have used to build successful and inclusive organizations. Their stories resonate in ways that theory alone cannot.

Students hear firsthand what it means to navigate professional environments where expectations are not always equal.
They gain insight into leadership journeys that differ from their own.
And they begin to understand the importance of perspective in shaping both opportunity and outcome.

These conversations often leave a lasting impression. They challenge assumptions. They broaden understanding. And they encourage students to think more deeply about the kind of leaders they want to become. Over time, I have come to see the classroom not just as a place of instruction, but as a place of formation.

A place where ideas are tested. Where perspectives are expanded. And where the foundation for future leadership begins to take shape.

Because in the end, leadership is not defined solely by strategy or financial performance. Those elements matter. But they are not sufficient on their own.

Leadership is defined by character. By the choices individuals make when faced with complexity. By how they treat others.
By the environments they create. And if students leave the classroom with a clearer understanding of that—if they begin their careers with an awareness of both the opportunity and the responsibility that leadership carries— Then the work we do in that space has lasting value.

Teaching has also expanded my own perspective in ways I did not fully anticipate. When I first entered the classroom, I assumed that much of my role would involve sharing what I had learned over the course of my career—translating experience into insight for students preparing to enter the professional world.

What I did not expect was how much I would continue to learn myself. Some of the most meaningful lessons have come not from textbooks or formal research, but from conversations—often informal, sometimes unexpected—with students and colleagues whose life experiences differ significantly from my own.

One of those moments came through my work with a graduate teaching assistant, Sai, who came from India. Through our conversations, I was introduced to perspectives that extended far beyond the scope of our coursework. Sai spoke about the complexities of the caste system in India—how it has shaped social structures, influenced opportunity, and affected the lived experiences of individuals across generations.

It was a reminder that systems of inequality are not confined to any one country or culture. They take different forms. They are shaped by different histories. But their impact is often similar.

Listening to Sai's experiences required me to step outside of my own frame of reference. To recognize that while I had spent years reflecting on issues of race and leadership within the United States, there were other systems—equally complex, equally influential—that I had only a limited understanding of.

That realization required humility. It required a willingness to listen without immediately interpreting. To ask questions without assuming understanding. And to accept that meaningful insight often comes from perspectives that challenge your own.

Every culture carries its own history of social divisions. Some are visible. Others are less apparent to those outside of that culture.

But in each case, those divisions shape access, opportunity, and the pathways available to individuals seeking to move forward.

Understanding those systems is not a simple task. It requires curiosity. It requires patience. And it requires a recognition that learning is ongoing—that no single experience or perspective provides a complete picture.

For me, these conversations reinforced an important lesson: Leadership in a global society demands more than technical skill or strategic thinking. It requires cultural awareness. It requires the ability to engage with people whose experiences differ from your own—not just at a surface level, but with a genuine interest in understanding how those experiences shape perspective. And it requires the discipline to approach those interactions thoughtfully. Not with assumptions. Not with quick conclusions. But with a willingness to listen and learn.

These lessons have influenced how I approach both teaching and leadership. In the classroom, they remind me that every student brings a unique set of experiences that shape how they see the world. Creating space for those perspectives is not simply inclusive—it is essential to meaningful learning.

Beyond the classroom, they reinforce the idea that leadership today operates within a broader, more interconnected environment than ever before. Organizations are no longer defined solely by local contexts. They are influenced by global markets, diverse workforces, and cultural dynamics that require thoughtful navigation.

Leaders who fail to recognize those realities risk misunderstanding the very environments they are responsible for guiding. But leaders who embrace that complexity—who are willing to learn, to listen, and to adapt—are better positioned to lead effectively in a changing world.

Looking back, it is striking how often the most important lessons come from places we do not expect. From conversations that were not planned. From perspectives we had not previously considered. From individuals who, in sharing their own stories, expand our understanding in ways that formal instruction alone cannot.

These interactions continue to remind me of something simple, yet essential: Learning is a lifelong process. It does not end with a degree.

It does not end with experience. It continues—through relationships, through curiosity, and through a willingness to remain open to what others can teach us.

KEY INSIGHT

The most effective leaders remain lifelong learners. They listen before they lead, seek understanding before judgment, and recognize that growth begins with humility.

Chapter 8

Alabama and the Weight of History

In 2025, I had the opportunity to participate in a service trip to Alabama through our church community. I had visited the South many times during my career, particularly during the years I lived and worked in Virginia. But this trip felt different from the beginning. The purpose was not professional, travel, or tourism. It was reflection and community outreach.

Our group planned to visit several historic sites connected to the Civil Rights Movement and the long history of racial injustice in the United States, including museums in both Birmingham and Montgomery. We also walked across the historic Edmund Pettis Bridge in Selma – site of "Bloody Sunday" in 1965.

Before the trip, I assumed I had a general understanding of that history. After all, I had read about slavery in school. I had watched documentaries. I had followed national conversations about race for decades. But standing in the places where those events unfolded would prove to be something very different from reading about them.

One of the most powerful moments of the trip occurred when we visited museums and memorials dedicated to the history of slavery and racial violence in America.

Walking into those spaces, I immediately sensed a different kind of atmosphere. Museums often present history in a way that feels distant—artifacts behind glass, timelines on the wall, carefully written descriptions that explain events long past.

But the exhibits we encountered in Alabama felt deeply personal. They told stories. Stories of families. Stories of individuals. Stories of lives interrupted by injustice.

One display described enslaved parents whose children were sold away from them. The language was simple, almost understated, but the emotional impact was overwhelming. I paused and tried to imagine the moment from a parent's perspective. A mother watching her child being taken away. A father powerless to intervene. A family permanently separated by the machinery of slavery.

The human cost of that reality is almost impossible to comprehend. Standing there, reading those accounts, I felt deep sadness. History suddenly felt very close.

Later, we visited the National Memorial for Peace and Justice. Walking through the memorial is a quiet, almost solemn experience. Large steel columns hang overhead, each one representing counties where documented lynchings occurred during the late nineteenth and early twentieth centuries.

Thousands of names are engraved on those structures. Names of individuals who were killed in acts of racial terror. Names of people whose lives were taken without trial, without justice, and often without any official acknowledgment at the time.

Visitors move slowly through the memorial. Some walk silently. Others pause to read the names. Occasionally, someone wipes away tears. The memorial does not shout its message. It simply presents the truth. And the truth carries its own weight.

Standing there, I felt the gravity of a history that many Americans—including myself for much of my life—had only partially understood.

For many years, the history of slavery and racial violence in America had felt somewhat distant to me. Not because I doubted its importance. But because the events existed in textbooks and documentaries rather than in my immediate experience. Walking through those memorials changed that. History stopped being abstract. It became personal. I began thinking about the generations of families whose lives were shaped by these events. The economic consequences. The social consequences. The emotional consequences.

The legacy of those experiences did not disappear when laws changed. They echoed forward through communities and generations. Standing in those memorial spaces, I realized something that had not fully registered before. The past is not as distant as we sometimes imagine. Its effects remain woven into the present.

As I walked through those exhibits, my mind drifted back to my childhood in Covington. I remember watching Clara arrive each Thursday morning on the bus. I remembered the neighborhoods divided by invisible lines. I remembered asking my mother why some houses looked different from others.

At the time, those differences seemed simple. Some people had more money. Some people had less. But standing in Alabama decades later, I began to see how incomplete that explanation had been. The economic and social patterns I observed as a child were connected to a much longer history. Policies. Practices. And injustices that stretched back generations. History had shaped those neighborhoods long before I noticed them. And in many ways, it continues shaping communities today.

There are moments in life when new information changes how we understand the past. And there are moments when experience itself reshapes our perspective.

The visit to Alabama was one of those experiences for me. Walking through the memorials and museums was emotionally difficult. At times, I felt sad. At times, I felt anger. At times, I felt a quiet sense of responsibility. Responsibility not for events that occurred long before I was born—but for understanding them honestly. History cannot be changed. But it can be acknowledged. And acknowledging it helps create the possibility of learning from it.

After visiting the memorials, our group gathered to talk about what we had seen. The conversations were thoughtful and sometimes emotional. People shared different reactions. Some expressed grief. Some expressed shock at details they had never previously encountered. Others spoke about how the experience deepened their commitment to justice and reconciliation.

Listening to those conversations reminded me again of something I had learned many times throughout my life. Understanding grows through dialogue. Through listening. Through allowing ourselves to encounter perspectives that may be uncomfortable. Growth rarely happens inside the boundaries of what already feels familiar.

When I left Alabama at the end of the trip, I carried with me a mixture of emotions. Sadness for the suffering that had occurred. Gratitude for the individuals who have worked to bring those stories to light. And a renewed sense of responsibility to continue learning.

Throughout my life, many experiences have gradually expanded my understanding of race and leadership. Friendships. Recovery meetings. Professional leadership roles. Teaching students from many backgrounds. The Alabama trip added another important piece to that journey.

It reminded me that understanding America's present requires acknowledging America's past. Not to dwell in guilt or resentment. But to learn. To grow. And to build communities where the dignity of every person is recognized.

As our bus headed up the interstate for the trip home, I looked out the window at the passing landscape. I found myself thinking about the many quiet experiences that had shaped my understanding of race over the years. Fields and towns stretched out across the horizon, quiet and peaceful. It was difficult to imagine that the same ground had once witnessed so much suffering.

Yet history often hides beneath the surface of everyday places. The trip strengthened something that had been growing inside me for many years. A commitment to keep encouraging conversations about leadership, opportunity, and human dignity. Not because those conversations are easy. But because they matter.

Understanding rarely arrives all at once. For me, it has come slowly. Through relationships. Through experience. Through moments—like that visit to Alabama—when history becomes impossible to ignore.

And perhaps that is part of the journey we all share. Learning. Listening. And continuing the work of building a more just and compassionate society. None of them seemed dramatic at the time.

A woman named Clara stepping off a bus to help my mother manage a house full of children.

A friend on a golf course explaining the subtle signals that determine whether someone feels welcome in a space.

Men and women sitting in a circle in an AA meeting, discovering that dignity does not depend on status or background.

Leadership meetings where different voices gradually changed the direction of an organization.

Students in a classroom wrestling with questions about responsibility and opportunity.

Each of those moments had seemed small on its own. But together they formed a kind of map. A map that slowly revealed how the invisible lines in our society affect the lives of real people.

Standing in Alabama, surrounded by reminders of the past, I realized that the journey of understanding is never really finished. History invites us to keep learning. And leadership, at its best, invites us to help create a future that reflects the dignity of every person.

As we left the final memorial site, there was a quietness among our group that did not require explanation. No one felt the need to fill the space with conversation. Some experiences speak for themselves.

What stayed with me most was not a single exhibit or moment, but a realization. Understanding history is not simply about learning what happened. It is about allowing those truths to shape how we see the present. And how we choose to move forward. Because once history becomes personal, it becomes harder to ignore. And much harder to forget.

When I returned home from Alabama, the experience stayed with me in ways I did not immediately expect. Days passed. Then weeks. And yet, moments from the visit would return—often without warning. Images from the memorials would surface in my mind. Rows of steel columns, suspended in quiet stillness. Each one bearing the names of individuals whose lives had been lost to racial violence.

The simplicity of the design made the weight of it even more powerful. Name after name. County after county. Story after story—most of them unknown to me, and in many cases, unknown to history. Those names represented lives that had been lived, families that had been affected, and stories that, in many cases, could no longer be told. And yet, the responsibility to remember them remained.

There was something about that experience that refused to be set aside. It did not offer easy conclusions. It did not resolve into a clear set of answers. Instead, it left me with a deeper awareness—one that had been forming over time, but now felt more defined.

The work of building understanding between people is never finished. It is not something that can be completed and set aside. It is ongoing. It is often difficult. And at times, it can feel overwhelming. But it is necessary. It requires humility—the willingness to recognize how much we do not fully understand. It requires courage—the willingness to engage in conversations that may feel uncomfortable or uncertain. And it requires persistence—the willingness to continue, even when progress feels slow.

In the weeks following that trip, I found myself reflecting on the path that had brought me to that moment. The experiences in Virginia. The work in the Midwest. The conversations in classrooms. The relationships formed through family, faith, and community.

Individually, each of those experiences had shaped my perspective in some way. But together, they began to form a pattern.

Looking back, I started to realize that many of the moments described throughout this book had been pointing in a similar direction all along. Not always clearly. Not always intentionally. But consistently.

They had drawn my attention to the importance of understanding. To the value of perspective. To the responsibility that comes with leadership—whether in organizations, communities, or personal relationships. Over time, that realization began to take on a different meaning.

What I had once thought of simply as an area of professional interest—diversity, inclusion, leadership development—began to feel like something more. It began to feel like a calling. Not a calling defined by position or title. But a calling shaped by opportunity.

Throughout my career, there were moments—some planned, many unexpected—when I found myself in a position to influence direction. Sometimes the role was small. Sometimes it carried greater responsibility. But the pattern was consistent.

Opportunities appeared to contribute—to help expand access, to encourage participation, to create space where it had not always existed. Often, I did not feel fully prepared for those moments.

There were times when I questioned whether I had the right experience, the right words, or the right approach. There were times when the path forward was not clear. But over time, I began to understand something about faith that had not always been obvious to me before. God does not always call the prepared. But He prepares the called.

Preparation, I came to realize, often happens in the process. It happens through experience. Through reflection.
Through stepping forward, even when the outcome is uncertain. Many times, the path only becomes visible after taking the first step. And once that step is taken, the next one begins to appear.

That lesson has shaped much of how I approach both leadership and life. It has taught me to pay attention to the opportunities in front of me—even when they feel unexpected.

To remain open to the possibility that the work I am being asked to do may be part of something larger than I can fully see. And to trust that growth often comes not from certainty, but from movement.

Looking back, I do not see a perfectly planned journey. I see a series of experiences—some chosen, some encountered—that, over time, have pointed in a consistent direction. Toward understanding. Toward connection. Toward the belief that people are meant to be seen, heard, and valued. And while the work itself is never finished, the responsibility to continue it remains. Not as an obligation alone. But as a calling.

One of the most challenging aspects of leadership is the uncertainty that accompanies change. Leaders are often called to move organizations forward—not when the path is fully defined, but when it is still taking shape. The destination may be clear in principle, but the route is rarely mapped out in detail.

That uncertainty can be unsettling. There is comfort in clarity. There is confidence in knowing what comes next. But leadership does not always offer that kind of assurance. More often, it asks for movement before certainty.

Throughout my career, I encountered many situations where the next step was not obvious. Moments when the questions outweighed the answers. When the risks felt real. When the possibility of failure was not just theoretical, but tangible.

In those moments, it would have been easy to wait. To gather more information. To seek greater consensus. To delay action until the path felt more certain. But over time, I began to understand something important: Waiting for complete certainty often prevents meaningful action. Opportunities do not always arrive fully formed. They often appear as possibilities—unfinished, unproven, and uncertain. And if leaders wait until every question is resolved, those opportunities can pass by.

This is where faith becomes essential. Faith can take different forms. For some, it is rooted in religious belief—a trust that guidance and purpose exist beyond what we can immediately see. For others, it is expressed through confidence in shared values, in the potential of people, or in the belief that progress is possible even when the outcome is not guaranteed.

In either case, faith requires movement. It requires the willingness to step forward without having every detail defined. To act not because the path is certain—but because the direction feels right.

Looking back, many of the most meaningful experiences of my life began that way. Not with a clear plan. But with a decision to move.

To accept a new role.
To start a conversation.
To pursue an idea.
To engage in work that carried both purpose and uncertainty.

Each of those steps led to something more. Not always in ways I expected. Not always without challenge. But consistently in ways that expanded my understanding and opened doors that would not have been visible otherwise. That is the nature of growth. It unfolds through action. It develops through experience. And it reveals itself over time—not all at once.

In my own life, this lesson has become deeply connected to my faith. There have been many moments when I did not feel fully prepared for what lay ahead. Moments when the direction was not entirely clear. Moments when taking a step forward required trust.

In those moments, I have come back to a simple belief: God does not require us to see the entire path. He asks us to take the next step. And often, it is only after that step is taken that the path begins to reveal itself. The next opportunity becomes visible. The next direction becomes clearer. The next step becomes possible.

This does not eliminate uncertainty. But it changes how we respond to it. Instead of waiting for clarity, we begin to move with purpose. Instead of being held back by doubt, we act with intention. Instead of focusing on what we cannot yet see, we focus on what we are being called to do now. That willingness to act—to take the first step—has shaped many of the opportunities I have experienced.

It has led to conversations that might not have happened. To roles I might not have pursued. To growth that would not have occurred if I had waited for certainty. And over time, it has reinforced a lesson that continues to guide me: You do not need to see the entire path to begin. You simply need the courage to take the first step. And trust that, in time, the steps that follow will be revealed.

My story about race is far from finished. In many ways, it feels like it is still unfolding—shaped by new experiences, new relationships, and new understandings that continue to develop over time. Like most people, I am still learning. That realization, once uncomfortable, has become something I now accept with a sense of humility. Because the truth is, understanding is not something we arrive at once and for all. It is something we grow into.

Over the years, that growth has been shaped by countless encounters—moments and relationships that, taken together, have expanded how I see the world and the people in it.

A woman named Clara, who rode the bus each week to help raise twelve children, showing quiet strength and dignity in ways I did not fully understand at the time.

Friends from college who introduced me to cultures beyond my own—broadening my perspective and challenging assumptions I had never thought to question.

Colleagues who helped me recognize subtle barriers within organizations—barriers that were not always visible, but were deeply felt by those navigating them.

Men and women in AA meetings who demonstrated, through honesty and vulnerability, that dignity has no social ranking—that every person carries value, regardless of circumstance.

Community leaders who showed me, through action, how diversity strengthens organizations—not as an abstract ideal, but as a practical and necessary reality.

Students who continue to challenge me—asking questions, offering perspectives, and reminding me that learning does not end with experience.

Each of these experiences widened my understanding of the human story. Not all at once. Not without moments of discomfort or reflection.

But steadily—through exposure, through relationships, and through a growing willingness to see beyond my own perspective. And the story continues. There are still conversations to be had. Still perspectives to understand. Still opportunities to listen, to learn, and to grow.

That ongoing nature of the journey is not a weakness. It is a strength. Because it keeps us open. Open to new ideas. Open to new relationships. Open to the possibility that there is always more to understand.

A friend once said something to me that has stayed with me for many years: "Wouldn't it be a boring world if we all looked and acted the same?" The simplicity of that statement carries a deeper truth. Our differences are not obstacles. They are invitations. Invitations to step beyond what is familiar. To engage with perspectives that challenge us. To recognize that the richness of human experience is found not in sameness, but in diversity.

When we begin to see differences in that way, something shifts. We move from hesitation to curiosity. From assumption to understanding. From distance to connection. And in doing so, we create the possibility for something greater.

Communities where people are not reduced to categories, but recognized as individuals. Organizations where diverse perspectives strengthen decision-making and expand opportunity. Relationships where respect and understanding replace fear and misunderstanding.

This vision is not fully realized. Not yet. But it is worth pursuing. The journey toward that vision is ongoing. It requires effort. It requires intention. And it requires individuals who are willing to participate—who are willing to take part in the work of building understanding, one conversation at a time.

Each of us has a role to play. Not because we have all the answers. But because we are part of the story. And the choices we make—how we listen, how we respond, how we engage with others—shape the direction that story takes.

Looking back, I do not see a single defining moment that changed everything. I see a series of moments. Small at the time. Significant in hindsight. Moments that, together, formed a path. A path that continues forward.

And while I do not know exactly where that path will lead, I have come to understand something that gives me confidence in taking the next step: That growth is always possible. That understanding can always deepen. And that the work of recognizing the dignity of every person is never complete—but always worth continuing.

The journey goes on.

And so do we.

KEY INSIGHT

Crossing lines—whether racial, cultural, economic, or personal—is ultimately about recognizing the dignity of every human being. The journey toward understanding is never finished, but every step matters.

The Innocence Project and the Pursuit of Justice

One of the most eye-opening experiences of my later years has come through service work in recovery. As part of my commitment to carrying the message of sobriety, I regularly participate in programs that bring recovery meetings into a county jail. Walking through those secure doors each week has given me a perspective on the criminal justice system that I never could have gained from reading reports or watching the news.

The men I meet come from many different backgrounds, but one reality is difficult to ignore: minority populations are often represented in numbers far greater than their share of the general community. Their stories are complex. Some made poor decisions. Some struggled with addiction, poverty, trauma, or mental illness. Yet many also describe experiences that raise troubling questions about fairness, opportunity, and equal treatment under the law.

These experiences led me to learn more about the work of the **Innocence Project**, a nonprofit organization dedicated to exonerating individuals who were wrongfully convicted of crimes. Through DNA testing, legal advocacy, and investigative work, the Innocence Project has helped free hundreds of people who spent years—and sometimes decades—in prison for crimes they did not commit.

What struck me most was not only the existence of wrongful convictions, but the patterns that often accompanied them. Studies have shown that minorities, particularly Black Americans, have been disproportionately affected by mistaken eyewitness identification, false confessions, inadequate legal representation, and systemic inequities within the justice system. While the vast majority of law enforcement officers, prosecutors, judges, and correctional professionals work honorably and conscientiously, the record demonstrates that no human institution is immune from error.

My experiences in county jail recovery meetings have reinforced a lesson I have learned repeatedly throughout life: systems are created by people, and people are imperfect. The goal is not to condemn institutions but to continually improve them. Organizations such as the Innocence Project remind us that justice is not simply about punishment; it is also about truth, accountability, and the willingness to correct mistakes when they occur.

The men I meet in recovery often speak about second chances. Recovery itself is built upon the belief that people can change, grow, and rebuild their lives. The same principle applies to institutions. A healthy society is one that continually examines itself, confronts uncomfortable realities, and strives to become fairer and more just.

My work in recovery has taught me that every person has a story. The more we listen to those stories, the more we recognize that human dignity extends beyond labels, past mistakes, or circumstances. Justice, at its best, honors that dignity and seeks not only accountability but also fairness, compassion, and truth.

KEY INSIGHT

Justice is strongest when it combines accountability with humility. The willingness to examine mistakes, correct injustices, and recognize the dignity of every individual strengthens both our institutions and our communities.

Epilogue

Crossing the Lines

Every now and then, I still think about Clara. Not in dramatic moments, but in quiet ones.

A city bus passes by on a neighborhood street. Someone folds a shirt with careful precision. A soft voice corrects a child with patient kindness. And suddenly I am back in that house in Covington, Kentucky.

The kitchen table is crowded. The washing machine hums down in the basement. Shoes and schoolbooks seem scattered across every room in the house. With twelve children, the house never really stood still.

Then the door opens.

Clara steps inside.

At the time, she was simply part of the rhythm of our family life. She arrived on Thursday mornings. She worked through the day. She helped my mother manage the impossible task of keeping a household of twelve children moving forward.

And in the late afternoon, she gathered her purse, walked down the block, and boarded the bus that carried her back to a world we never saw.

As a child, I never thought much about that bus ride.

It was simply how Clara arrived.

And how she left.

But as the years have passed, that bus ride has taken on a different meaning in my mind.

Clara crossed lines every Thursday.

Lines between neighborhoods.

Lines between opportunity and limitation.

Lines between lives that touched briefly but rarely overlapped.

At the time, I could not see those lines.

Like many children, I lived inside the small world I knew. My understanding of the country—of race, opportunity, and history—was narrow and incomplete.

But life has a way of expanding our perspective. Sometimes slowly. Sometimes, through experiences we never expected.

Over the years, my life carried me across many of those invisible lines.

I crossed them when I walked into my first Alcoholics Anonymous meeting and discovered a room where a bank president and a homeless man shared the same dignity.

I crossed them when friendships revealed experiences very different from my own.

I crossed them in leadership roles in my professional life, where organizations began learning that inclusion makes communities stronger.

I crossed them in classrooms where students from many cultures gathered to prepare for the responsibilities of business leadership.

And I crossed them again years later while standing in Alabama, surrounded by memorials that forced me to confront a painful chapter of our nation's history.

Each experience widened the lens through which I saw the world.

Each encounter reminded me that the stories we inherit are only part of the truth.

The rest we discover through relationships.

Through listening.

It takes quiet courage to step beyond what is familiar.

Looking back now, I realize that the journey described in this book did not begin with a leadership position or a classroom lecture.

It began with something much simpler.

A bus ride.

A woman who showed up each week to help a large family manage the demands of everyday life.

Clara never lectured us about justice.

She never spoke about social systems or historical patterns.

She simply lived with dignity.

She worked hard.

She treated everyone around her with patience and kindness.

And in ways I could not possibly understand as a young boy, she became part of the foundation that would eventually shape my understanding of humanity.

Years later, I sometimes wonder about Clara's life beyond the bus ride to our house.

Did she have children who watched her leave early in the morning for work?

Did she sit quietly by a window during the ride home after a long day of helping raise someone else's family?

Did she ever wonder what paths the children in our house would follow as they grew older?

Those are questions I will never be able to answer. But I do know this. Her presence mattered. She was one of the first people who quietly crossed the lines that divided the world I knew. And because of that, she helped open the door to a journey of understanding that has lasted a lifetime.

A friend once said something that has stayed with me for many years. "Wouldn't it be a boring world if we all looked and acted the same?" He was right. The richness of life comes from the variety of human experiences.

Different cultures.

Different traditions.

Different stories.

Each one adds depth to the larger story of humanity.

The older I become, the more I realize that learning never truly ends.

Each new generation brings different questions.

Each new relationship offers another opportunity to understand the world more fully.

Each new encounter reminds us that the story of humanity is still unfolding. Perhaps the most important lesson I have learned is this:

The lines that divide us are often not as permanent as they appear.

Sometimes they exist in geography.

Sometimes in history.

Sometimes, in our assumptions about one another.

But those lines can be crossed.

They can become places where curiosity replaces fear.

Where conversation replaces silence.

Where understanding begins.

Every Thursday morning long ago, a bus carried Clara across town to our house in Covington. At the time, I thought it was simply part of the routine of our family life. Now I understand it differently.

That bus was carrying a lesson I would spend the rest of my life learning. The lines that divide us are often invisible—until someone quietly crosses them. And when they do, the journey toward understanding begins. And that's where we begin, step by step, to cross over into a deeper understanding of one another.

The bus that carried Clara across town every Thursday morning also carried a lesson I would spend a lifetime learning. The lines that divide us are often invisible—until someone quietly crosses them. Clara showed me how to do that.

If there is one thing I have come to believe, it is this: Understanding is rarely the result of a single moment. It is built over time. Through relationships. Through experiences. Through the willingness to notice what we once overlooked.

Clara's bus ride did not seem extraordinary at the time. But in many ways, it was the beginning of everything that followed.

A quiet crossing.

A simple act.

A moment that would take decades to fully understand.

And perhaps that is how most journeys begin.

Not with answers.

But with something we do not yet fully see.

The journey I have described is personal.
But the questions it raises do not belong to me alone. If there is one lesson that has stayed with me over the course of this journey, it is this: understanding is not a destination. It is a responsibility.

Each generation inherits a world shaped by the decisions, assumptions, and actions of those who came before. We do not choose the starting point. But we do choose what we do with it.

Today, conversations about race, opportunity, and human dignity often feel complicated. At times, they can feel overwhelming. At other times, they can feel divisive. People approach these issues from different experiences, different histories, and different perspectives. It is not surprising that disagreement exists.

But disagreement does not eliminate responsibility.

Leadership—whether in a boardroom, a classroom, a workplace, or a family—requires more than technical skill or professional expertise. It requires awareness. It requires humility. And perhaps most importantly, it requires the willingness to keep learning.

For many years, I believed that understanding came from having the right answers. Over time, I have come to believe something different. Understanding begins with the willingness to ask better questions. It begins with listening. Leadership today carries a unique challenge.

We live in a time when information is constant, opinions are immediate, and conversations can quickly become polarized. It is easy to retreat into familiar viewpoints or surround ourselves with voices that reinforce what we already believe.

But leadership calls us to do something more difficult. It calls us to engage. To remain open. To recognize that the experiences of others may differ from our own in ways we have not fully considered.

In my own life, some of the most important lessons did not come from formal training or structured programs. They came from relationships. From conversations. From moments when I realized that someone else's experience of the same environment was very different from mine.

Those moments were not always comfortable. But they were necessary. Leadership requires the courage to remain present in those moments. Not to solve every issue immediately. Not to have all the answers. But to stay engaged long enough to understand. Because understanding is the foundation of meaningful action.

Listening is often described as a simple skill. In reality, it is one of the most difficult disciplines we can practice. Most of us listen with the intention of responding. We prepare our thoughts while the other person is still speaking. We filter what we hear through our own experiences, our own assumptions, and our own expectations. True listening asks something different of us. It asks us to pause. To set aside, even temporarily, the need to evaluate or respond. To hear not only the words being spoken, but the experience behind them.

Over the years, I have learned that some of the most important insights in my life came when I stopped trying to interpret another person's story through my own lens—and simply allowed it to stand on its own.

Listening does not require agreement. It requires respect. It requires the recognition that every person carries a story shaped by experiences we may never fully see. When we listen with that mindset, something begins to change.

Conversations become less about winning and more about understanding. And understanding opens the door to connection. The idea of building understanding can feel abstract. But in reality, it often begins with small, everyday choices. Simple actions. Consistent habits. Intentional decisions about how we engage with the people around us.

Here are a few practices that have shaped my own journey:

1. Be Curious About People's Stories
Take the time to ask questions. Not out of obligation, but out of genuine curiosity. Every person you encounter carries experiences that have shaped how they see the world.

2. Step Outside Familiar Circles
Growth rarely happens in environments where everyone shares the same background or perspective. Seek opportunities to build relationships with people whose experiences differ from your own.

3. Pay Attention to What You Have Not Had to Notice
One of the most powerful shifts in my life came when I began recognizing the things I had never needed to think about. Awareness often begins by noticing what has previously gone unseen.

4. Choose Conversations Over Assumptions
It is easy to form opinions from a distance. It is harder—but far more valuable—to engage in thoughtful conversation. When possible, replace assumptions with dialogue.

5. Lead Where You Are
Leadership is not limited to formal titles. It exists in everyday interactions—with colleagues, students, family members, and

neighbors. The way we treat people, the way we listen, and the way we respond all shape the environments around us.

6. Stay Committed to the Process
Understanding does not arrive all at once. It develops over time. There will be moments of clarity, but also moments of uncertainty. The goal is not perfection. The goal is progress.

As I reflect on the journey described in this book, I am reminded again that the most meaningful lessons did not come from extraordinary moments.

They came from ordinary encounters.

A conversation on a golf course.

A meeting in a church basement.

A leadership discussion in a boardroom.

A visit to a place where history still speaks.

And long ago, a woman stepping off a bus and walking into our home. Each of those moments carried an invitation.

An invitation to notice.

To listen.

To learn.

That invitation is still present. Not just for me, but for all of us. The work of building understanding is not reserved for a particular profession, position, or stage of life. It is part of what it means to live in a community with others.

It is part of what it means to lead. And it is part of what it means to grow.

Where we go from here is not determined by a single decision or a single moment. It is shaped by the choices we make each day. The questions we are willing to ask. The conversations we are willing to enter. And the people we are willing to truly see.

The lines that once seemed fixed are not as permanent as they appear. They can be crossed. One conversation at a time. One relationship at a time. One step at a time.

And perhaps that is how change has always happened.

Quietly.

Gradually.

Through people who are willing to listen—and willing to move forward together. The lines are still there. The question is whether we are willing to see them—and step across them. Only then will a transformation occur.

FINAL REFLECTION

The goal of this journey is not perfection. It is progress. Every relationship that broadens our perspective, every conversation that deepens understanding, and every act of empathy helps build a more just and compassionate world. The lines that once separated us become bridges when we choose to cross them.

Historical Civil Rights Sites

Civil Rights Landmarks in America

Places That Help Tell the Story

Across the United States, numerous historic locations preserve the stories of individuals and communities who helped transform the nation during the Civil Rights Movement. Visiting these sites offers a powerful opportunity to understand the courage, sacrifice, and determination required to challenge systems of racial injustice.

Many of the places listed below played a direct role in shaping the modern Civil Rights Movement. Others preserve earlier chapters of the struggle for freedom and equality in America. Together, they help tell the larger story of how the nation has wrestled with questions of justice, opportunity, and human dignity.

Alabama: Key Sites of the Civil Rights Movement

National Memorial for Peace and Justice
417 Caroline Street
Montgomery, Alabama 36104

Often called the National Lynching Memorial, this powerful site commemorates thousands of African Americans who were victims of racial terror lynchings between 1877 and 1950. Large steel columns hang overhead, each engraved with the names of victims and the counties where the violence occurred.

The memorial invites visitors to confront a painful chapter of American history and to reflect on the continuing pursuit of justice.

Legacy Museum: From Enslavement to Mass Incarceration
400 North Court Street
Montgomery, Alabama 36104

Located near the memorial, the Legacy Museum traces the history of racial injustice in the United States from slavery through the era of segregation and into the modern criminal justice system. Through immersive exhibits and historical documentation, the museum illustrates how systems of inequality developed and how their effects continue to shape American society.

Dexter Avenue King Memorial Baptist Church
454 Dexter Avenue
Montgomery, Alabama 36104

Dexter Avenue King Memorial Baptist Church was the pastoral home of Dr. Martin Luther King Jr. from 1954 to 1960. From this church, King helped lead the Montgomery Bus Boycott, one of the earliest and most important victories of the Civil Rights Movement.

The church stands only a short distance from the Alabama State Capitol, symbolizing the movement's challenge to long-standing systems of segregation and injustice.

Rosa Parks Statue
Alabama State Capitol Grounds
600 Dexter Avenue
Montgomery, Alabama 36104

This statue honors Rosa Parks, whose refusal to give up her seat on a segregated bus in 1955 helped spark the Montgomery Bus Boycott. Her quiet act of courage became a turning point in American history and helped launch a national movement demanding equal rights and dignity for African Americans.

Civil Rights Memorial
400 Washington Avenue
Montgomery, Alabama 36104

Designed by artist Maya Lin, the Civil Rights Memorial honors forty individuals who lost their lives during the struggle for civil rights between 1954 and 1968. Water flows across a circular granite monument engraved with the names of those who died in the movement, symbolizing the ongoing pursuit of justice.

Edmund Pettus Bridge
Broad Street & Water Avenue
Selma, Alabama 36701

The Edmund Pettus Bridge became a symbol of the Civil Rights Movement during the Selma to Montgomery marches of 1965. On March 7 of that year, known as Bloody Sunday, peaceful demonstrators were violently attacked by state troopers as they attempted to cross the bridge to demand voting rights. Images from the attack shocked the nation and helped lead to the passage of the Voting Rights Act of 1965.

Birmingham Civil Rights Institute
520 16th Street North
Birmingham, Alabama 35203

Located across from the historic 16th Street Baptist Church, this museum documents the struggle for civil rights in Birmingham during the 1950s and 1960s. Exhibits explore the 1963 Birmingham Campaign, when peaceful protesters, including schoolchildren, were met with police dogs and fire hoses. These events helped galvanize national support for the Civil Rights Act of 1964.

16th Street Baptist Church
1530 16th Street North
Birmingham, Alabama 35203

This church became the site of a tragic act of racial violence when a bombing on September 15, 1963, killed four young African American girls. The attack shocked the nation and intensified support for civil rights legislation.

National Civil Rights Landmarks

Martin Luther King Jr. National Historical Park
450 Auburn Avenue NE
Atlanta, Georgia 30312

This historic district includes the birth home of Dr. Martin Luther King Jr., Ebenezer Baptist Church, where he preached, and the King Center, where he and Coretta Scott King are buried. The site preserves the legacy of one of the most influential leaders of the Civil Rights Movement.

National Civil Rights Museum
450 Mulberry Street
Memphis, Tennessee 38103

Located at the former Lorraine Motel, where Dr. Martin Luther King Jr. was assassinated in 1968, the museum traces the history of the Civil Rights Movement from slavery through modern times.

Little Rock Central High School National Historic Site
2120 West Daisy L. Gatson Bates Drive
Little Rock, Arkansas 72202

In 1957, nine African American students, now known as the Little Rock Nine, integrated this previously all-White high school under the protection of federal troops. Their courage became a defining moment in the struggle to implement the Supreme Court's decision in *Brown v. Board of Education.*

Brown v. Board of Education National Historical Park
1515 Southeast Monroe Street
Topeka, Kansas 66612

This site commemorates the landmark 1954 Supreme Court decision declaring racially segregated public schools unconstitutional. The ruling became one of the most significant legal milestones of the Civil Rights Movement.

Why These Places Matter

Civil rights landmarks are more than historical sites. They are places where the nation confronted some of its deepest moral challenges.

Civil Rights History in the Cincinnati–Northern Kentucky Region

While many of the most widely known civil rights events occurred in the American South, the struggle for freedom and equality has deep roots in communities across the Midwest. Cities along the Ohio River, including Cincinnati, Covington, and Newport, played important roles in earlier movements for freedom and justice.

National Underground Railroad Freedom Center
50 East Freedom Way
Cincinnati, Ohio 45202

Located along the banks of the Ohio River, this museum stands on ground that once marked the boundary between slave states and free states. The Freedom Center tells the story of the Underground Railroad and explores the continuing struggle for freedom and human rights.

Harriet Beecher Stowe House
2950 Gilbert Avenue
Cincinnati, Ohio 45206

Harriet Beecher Stowe lived in Cincinnati while writing *Uncle Tom's Cabin*, the influential novel that exposed the brutality of slavery to millions of readers. Her experiences in the border city helped shape a book that energized the abolitionist movement.

John Rankin House
6152 Rankin Hill Road
Ripley, Ohio 45167

Overlooking the Ohio River, the Rankin House served as a critical station on the Underground Railroad. Reverend John Rankin and his family helped hundreds of enslaved people escape to freedom. A lantern placed in the window often guided freedom seekers crossing the river from Kentucky.

Lincoln Grant School Historic Site
824 Greenup Street
Covington, Kentucky 41011

The Lincoln Grant School was one of Covington's historically Black schools during the era of segregation. The school reflects an important chapter in the educational history of Northern Kentucky and the resilience of communities seeking opportunity despite unequal systems.

James Baldwin Statue
Ohio Riverfront, Covington, Kentucky

This statue honors James Baldwin, one of America's most influential writers and voices on race, identity, and human dignity. While Baldwin's national legacy is rooted in his powerful essays and speeches, his presence in Covington serves as a symbolic connection between the region and the broader national conversation on race and justice. The statue stands as a reminder that the work of understanding, through storytelling, reflection, and honest dialogue, is essential to building more inclusive communities.

Theodore M. Berry International Friendship Park
925 Riverside Drive
Cincinnati, Ohio 45202

Named after Cincinnati's first African American mayor, Theodore Berry, this riverfront park celebrates global understanding and cultural diversity. Berry was a civil rights advocate and community leader whose career reflected a commitment to expanding opportunity and representation in public life.

Union Baptist Church
405 West 7th Street
Cincinnati, Ohio 45203

Founded in 1831, Union Baptist Church is one of the oldest African American congregations west of the Allegheny Mountains. The church played an active role in the Underground Railroad and served as a center for abolitionist activity and community leadership.

Allen Temple AME Church
7080 Reading Road
Cincinnati, Ohio 45237

Allen Temple AME Church has long served as a center of spiritual life, civil rights advocacy, and community organization in Cincinnati. Like many AME churches, it has played an important role in advancing education, civic engagement, and social justice.

Manse Hotel and Annex (Historic Site)
906–910 Chapel Street
Cincinnati, Ohio 45206

During the era of segregation, the Manse Hotel provided accommodations for African American travelers who were denied access to other hotels. It hosted prominent entertainers, athletes, and leaders, making it an important cultural landmark in Cincinnati's Black history.

Newport Southbank Bridge ("Purple People Bridge")
Connecting Cincinnati, Ohio, and Newport, Kentucky

Now a pedestrian bridge, this crossing symbolizes the historic connection between free and slave states along the Ohio River. For many escaping slavery, the river represented both a barrier and a gateway to freedom.

Visiting these locations reminds us that many of the freedoms Americans enjoy today were achieved through the courage of individuals who refused to accept injustice as permanent. These sites invite reflection, dialogue, and continued commitment to building communities that recognize the dignity and equality of every person.

The following sources informed the historical context and leadership perspectives referenced throughout this memoir.

References & Resources

Alexander, M. (2010). *The New Jim Crow: Mass incarceration in the age of colorblindness.* The New Press.

Baldwin, J. (1963). *The fire next time.* Dial Press.

Berry, T. M. (1970). *Black political leadership in Cincinnati.* Cincinnati Urban League.

Branch, T. (1988). *Parting the waters: America in the King years, 1954–1963.* Simon & Schuster.

Brown v. Board of Education, 347 U.S. 483 (1954).

Carson, C. (Ed.). (1998). *The autobiography of Martin Luther King, Jr.* Warner Books.

Civil Rights Act of 1964, Pub. L. No. 88-352, 78 Stat. 241.

Du Bois, W. E. B. (1903). *The souls of Black folk.* A.C. McClurg & Co.

Equal Justice Initiative. (2017). *Lynching in America: Confronting the legacy of racial terror.* Equal Justice Initiative.

Fair Housing Act of 1968, Pub. L. No. 90-284, 82 Stat. 73.

Hofstede, G. (2001). *Culture's consequences: Comparing values, behaviors, institutions and organizations across nations* (2nd ed.). Sage Publications.

King, M. L., Jr. (1963). *Letter from Birmingham Jail.*

King, M. L., Jr. (1964). *Why we can't wait.* Harper & Row.

Kendi, I. X. (2019). *How to be an antiracist.* One World.

Putnam, R. D. (2000). *Bowling alone: The collapse and revival of American community.* Simon & Schuster.

Rothstein, R. (2017). *The color of law: A forgotten history of how our government segregated America.* Liveright Publishing.

Sugrue, T. J. (2014). *The origins of the urban crisis: Race and inequality in postwar Detroit.* Princeton University Press.

U.S. Department of Housing and Urban Development. (n.d.). *History of fair housing.* https://www.hud.gov

Alcoholics Anonymous World Services. (2001). *Alcoholics Anonymous* (4th ed.). AA World Services.

Alcoholics Anonymous World Services. (1953). *Twelve steps and twelve traditions.* AA World Services.

Foundational Archives & Digital Collections

- Library of Congress Civil Rights Resources — One of the strongest starting points for primary documents, speeches, photographs, oral histories, and teaching resources.
- National Archives Civil Rights Collection — Includes Rosa Parks' arrest records, Voting Rights Act materials, FBI files, court documents, and federal civil rights records.
- Civil Rights Digital Library — A major digital portal connecting archives, museums, television footage, and historical collections nationwide.
- Civil Rights Movement Archive — Particularly valuable because it preserves the movement "from the perspective of those who were there," including firsthand accounts, letters, speeches, and movement documents.

- Stanford King Institute Papers Project — Comprehensive archive of speeches, sermons, correspondence, and writings of Martin Luther King Jr.

Museums

National Civil Rights Museum

Located at the former Lorraine Motel, where Martin Luther King Jr. was assassinated. Excellent educational exhibits and student resources.
National Civil Rights Museum

National Museum of African American History and Culture

Part of the Smithsonian, one of the premier repositories for African American and civil rights history.
Smithsonian NMAAHC

The King Center

Focused on nonviolence, leadership, and the legacy of Dr. King.
The King Center

Amistad Research Center

One of the nation's most important archives documenting African American history and the modern Civil Rights Movement.
Amistad Research Center

Best Books on Civil Rights History

General Movement Histories

- Parting the Waters by Taylor Branch
- Bearing the Cross by David Garrow
- The Strange Career of Jim Crow by C. Vann Woodward
- Eyes on the Prize by Juan Williams

Memoirs & Firsthand Accounts

- The Autobiography of Malcolm X
- Walking with the Wind by John Lewis
- Coming of Age in Mississippi by Anne Moody

Modern Interpretations

- The New Jim Crow by Michelle Alexander
- Caste by Isabel Wilkerson

Documentary Films & Video Resources

- Eyes on the Prize — Widely considered the definitive documentary series on the Civil Rights Movement.
- PBS Civil Rights Collection — Documentary clips, interviews, timelines, and educational material.
- Selma — Focused on the Selma voting rights campaign.
- Freedom Riders — Excellent documentary on interracial activism during desegregation efforts.

Educational & Teaching Resources

- Zinn Education Project – Civil Rights Movement — Strong classroom-ready lesson plans, readings, and activities.
- SNCC Digital Gateway — Excellent for studying the Student Nonviolent Coordinating Committee and grassroots activism.
- Teaching for Change Civil Rights Resources — Primary documents and classroom materials.

Topics Beyond the Traditional Narrative

Many newer resources expand beyond the familiar focus on Dr. King and the 1950s–60s South:

- Women in the movement (e.g., Ella Baker, Fannie Lou Hamer)
- Northern civil rights activism
- Labor and economic justice
- Student activism and SNCC
- LGBTQ contributions, including Bayard Rustin
- Hispanic, Native American, Asian American, disability-rights, and women 's-rights movements are connected to broader civil rights history.

About the Author

Dr. Dan Dressman is an educator, leadership consultant, and former association executive. He serves as an Assistant Professor of Management at the University of Cincinnati's Lindner College of Business. Throughout his career, he has worked with professional associations and leadership initiatives focused on strengthening organizations, breaking down barriers, and expanding opportunity.

www.ingramcontent.com/pod-product-compliance
Lightning Source LLC
LaVergne TN
LVHW040223110826
845146LV00004B/1269

* 9 7 9 8 9 9 4 9 8 1 8 3 2 *